FERNANDO R

THE FINAL BATTLE

Part of the proceeds will go to The Rangers Charity Foundation

RANGERS
CHARITY
FOUNDATION

FERNANDO RICKSEN
THE FINAL BATTLE
Life with MND

WITH VINCENT DE VRIES & VERONIKA RICKSEN

TRANSLATED BY MICHIEL BLIJBOOM

First published in Great Britain in 2020 by
VCT Media

ISBN: 978-9-08230-161-8
eBook ISBN: 978-9-08230-166-3

First published in the Netherlands in 2020 by Kosmos Uitgevers as
Fernando Ricksen - De Finale Strijd - Leven met ALS

Cover photo by Goffe Struiksma

Design and typeset by Ellis Ketels

Production by Michiel Holsheimer

Printed by New Energy

VCT MEDIA

CONTENTS

'Whatever happens, please finish the book!'

Fernando Ricksen, 2017

PROLOGUE

"Is he heavy?" asks Veronika.

"Yeah, quite heavy," is my response, via WhatsApp. "At least six pounds. Maybe even close to ten."

"Must be his porcelain teeth then."

Veronika, the Russian beauty whom Fernando married way back in 2014, makes the joke. But I immediately think: it's the kind of wisecrack that he *could* have made. Straightforward, just like the kinda guy he was.

Remember that this was the guy who was in stitches when he saw what kind of Xmas present his team mates had bought for David Murray, the filthy rich chairman of, then, Glasgow Rangers. A pair of socks. Not very fitting (pun intended) for a guy with no legs...

But Fernando isn't laughing anymore. He is not even alive anymore. More to the point: his ashes are in my backpack. Stored inside the urn with which I walk through the streets of Glasgow, a mere nine weeks since the footballer kicked the proverbial bucket. And that is not something to laugh about. The universe seems to agree with me, as today it is cold, wet and windy. But on the other hand: that's Scotland.

It's weird, to say the least, to walk around with the remains of what has been one of my best friends ever. Words basically fail me to describe the feeling. But at the same time it's beautiful. I really feel honoured that I have been chosen to pick him up. Veronika asked me to do it. Collect what's left of her husband, in the city that brought him so much. Yes, I feel privileged. And I would never have said no. This, no matter how bizarre, is the kind of things you do for a friend. And Fernando Ricksen, once again, was my friend.

So here I am, in Glasgow, that wonderful city on the banks of the river Clyde. The city where Fernando was seen as a hero, a hero with a fighting spirit. Especially after his active career as a footballer, when he was trying to tackle the deadly disease MND. Maybe that's when he got the most recognition. When he was battling with an opponent who, as yet, nobody has ever beaten. The Scots, especially the red, white & blue ones, used a word for it that sums it up completely. That word, of course, is Braveheart.

No other place in the world could have been a better choice for a great send-off. This is where people cheered for Fernando when he hit a ball (and sometimes an opponent) on behalf of Rangers. And this is where the same people – plus the green and white ones! – cheered for him on the 25th of September 2019, the day his dead body was driven around. A week earlier, the 43-year old Dutchman had finally succumbed to one of the dirtiest diseases in the history of mankind. I once said that Fernando's funeral was a bit like Princess Di's. Okay, I exaggerated a little. But just a little. No, it wasn't millions of mourners, but at least thousands and thousands. Which, at the time, felt like millions. I still remember the farewell salute in front of Rangers' stadium, executed by Steven Gerrard and the entire Rangers squad. Goosebumps. And no, not just because of the Scottish weather.

Just like in 1997, with the people's Princess, red roses and stuffed toys were thrown upon the hearse. For a moment, nobody cared about the descent or religion of the person next to them. The entire lot were united, connected by the same appreciation and compassion.

I had already noticed that, many months earlier. A Celtic pennant, hanging on the wall of his room in St Andrew's Hospice in Airdrie. Sent to him by a Hoops fan. It came with a letter, in which the guy wrote that he hated and cursed Fernando in his time as a Gers ace. But that all that anger and rage had been replaced by respect. Respect for the way the dying Dutchman was handling MND. It was something he wanted to let him know. Hence the pennant.

And this guy wasn't the only Bhoy who suddenly supported him. Because apart from Rangers faces like Michael Mols, Nacho Novo, Thomas Buffel, Marvin Andrews, Billy Dodds, Allan McGregor, Tore Andre Flo, Neil McCann, Marco Negri, Arthur Numan, Steven Thompson, Steven Gerrard, Ally McCoist, Mark Hateley, Andy Goram, Richard Gough, John Brown and Ian Durrant, there were also people like Celtic chairman Ian Bankier, Celtic manager Neil Lennon and former

Celtic player Bobby Petta who sang 'Will your anchor hold in the storms of life', as people paid tribute to the late Fernando under the roof of Wellington Church in Hillhead.

"The rivalry is here to stay," Petta later said. "But Fernando has been responsible for closing the gap a little bit. At least through him, some respect for the opponent has emerged. That's what Fernando has achieved. And in a divided city like Glasgow, that's quite something."

Fernando the bridge builder. It takes a bit of time to get used to the idea. Because, let's face it, as a footballer he wasn't exactly what one calls a peace keeper. On the contrary! Whenever and wherever a fight occurred, the Dutch defender was on the frontline. And quite often he was the one who had *caused* all the trouble. Yes, he could be an idiot. He knew it, we all knew it. And for sure Vladislav Radimov does. A former team mate at Zenit Saint Petersburg, he was knocked down by Fernando during a friendly (!) in Malaga. Just like that. His Russian wasn't probably up to standard, so Mr Ricksen let his granite fist do the talking.

Only in Russia? Not really. I remember he once told me how he gave a Celtic fan a good hiding, just off Sauchiehall Street. The guy had been calling him names – and spat at him. So he knocked the shit out of him, just to set the record straight. Fernando Ricksen wasn't much of a talker.

Out of respect for this anonymous Celts fan, I skip the little side street on my walk with Fernando's ashes. And no, me and the ashes aren't visiting [strip joint] Seventh Heaven either. Fernando used to love that lap dance bar on Newton Terrace.

Remember the guy who used to turn off the lights at the end of a hot and steamy night? It was the captain of Glasgow Rangers, AKA Fernando Jacob Hubertina Henrika Ricksen.

Oh, he would have loved it, no doubt about it! He would have applauded the idea of the urn with his mortal remains (and the porcelain teeth!) being placed on a table, surrounded by a fine selection of scantily clad, big breasted representants of the opposite sex. But no, I prefer to take his ashes to the little square that has been named after that other bridge builder, Nelson Mandela. Also because that's close to where my hotel is. Or should I say: *our* hotel?

The next morning I take a taxi to the airport. But I ask the driver to take a bit of a scenic route. Normally one uses the M8 to Paisley, across Kingston Bridge, and then via exit 28 the journey continues to where the planes are. But no, I now want to take exit 24 already, which leads us to Helen Street.

Yes, we're on our way to Ibrox, the brick red football cathedral where for six long seasons Fernando brought pleasure to the masses. If you supported Rangers, that is. "He never gave up. That's why I love the guy so much," die-hard Rangers fan Brian Donnelly once told me. I met Donnelly nine weeks ago, at Fernando's big send-off. He had to be there, he told me. He, the father of two year old Rixon, who was named after... You get it. Back then, on that memorable 25th of September, Donnelly told me a horrible story. How he had shivers when he heard that Fernando would be taken to the same crematorium that he, Brian Donnelly, had visited a year earlier, with his stillborn daughter.

It's quiet now, on Edmiston Drive. A complete contrast to the situation nine weeks ago, when it was so bloody crowded that people had to climb into trees and lantern poles in order to catch a glimpse of Fernando's funeral procession. And now, there is nobody. Just me, a cab driver and what's left of Fernando.

If I try hard enough, I can still hear Connor Honeyball of CWH Piping and Craig Lawrie of The Paisley Pipers, belting out 'Farewell to Govan'. If I squeeze my eyes, I can imagine that I still see the thousands of shirts, balloons, scarves, photo's, flags, poems that were here, on the pavement and on the fence, to pay tribute to the lost Ranger. But they've gone. All that's left, are memories.

"Can you please stop here, for a moment?" I ask the driver. His foot touches the brake pedal. And we come to a halt, me and Fernando. Right in front of the Ibrox Disaster Memorial.

This is it.

This is the moment.

The moment for Fernando to finally say farewell to his beloved Ibrox. I grab my backpack and lift it. Hold it towards the stadium. And I am quiet, for ten long seconds.

"Okay, you can go now," I then say to the driver. Because we're done here. Fernando has paid his tribute. The lap of honour is finished. Fernando can go home.

At the airport, I have to hand over the ashes at security. It's a weird idea: for years and years Fernando has travelled business class, but his final flight is as hand luggage.

"What is that?" says the security guard who grabs the urn.

And, as he sees the FR2 inscription on it: "Is that Fernando?"

"Yes," I answer.

All of a sudden the guard's eyes are filled with tears. "I am a massive Rangers fan," he then says. "And this guy meant a lot to me."

***

Ten weeks later. The sky blue urn with Fernando's remains is in Veronika's hands. Veronika is in De Baandert, the neighbourhood that has given its name to the old ground of Fortuna Sittard, Fernando's first – and last – professional football club. More precisely, Veronika is at RK Urnenhof, the former Bernadette Church, where dean Wilbert van Rens has just praised Fernando for the fighting spirit he has shown during, and especially after his footballing days. It's quiet, in these holy surroundings. But Veronika swears she hears Fernando chuckle. Somewhere up there, on his cloud. Because for her he is still around, although she can't see him.

She's always had that feeling, right from the moment he died, five months ago. All those little signs. Her flight number when she went to Glasgow for his memorial service, started with his initials, FR. Her seat number: 2, the same one he had on his shirt. Those were signs, she was convinced of that. On the flight back to Valencia, she once again had seat number 2. A coincidence? No way!

It feels weird, she has to admit as the urn, together with a drawing from daughter Isabella, is put away for ten years. But it also feels good. Because she knows that this is the place where Fernando wanted to be put to rest. Here, in the Dutch town of Sittard, where his football adventure really began. Just like Fernando, the old Fortuna stadium has gone. Where he once defended the club colours of yellow and green are houses now, in which families live their happy little lives. In other words: it's history. Football history. But so is Fernando. Therefore it's a perfect spot for him to rest in peace. Here, where to the people who know, it will always smell of grass.

Vincent de Vries, June 2020

2013: The Denial

SEPTEMBER 26, 2013: **Death sentence**

"Hey Vincent, I have to tell you something."

"What's up?"

"I told you about my sore back, right?"

I nod.

"And I also told you that I thought it was about that previous hernia, remember?"

Once again I nod.

"Well, it's not. It's something else. I have MND. At least: they *think* I have MND."

He is serious. Dead serious. This is not the Fernando Ricksen I know. He even whispers, at times. The bravado has gone. He tells me that he has visited a neurologist. Edwin Jansen, Fortuna Sittard's club doctor, had told him to do so. Jansen simply didn't trust it. He had seen how Fernando walked and talked during and after the testimonial for his former team mate Mark van Bommel. It didn't feel good, to him. It was suspicious. Hence the advice to see a specialist.

"Obviously it came as a complete shock. But the worst bit of it all was..."

He pauses.

I say nothing.

"...the way he said it. Stone cold."

"What do you mean?"

"He didn't wrap it in words, you know. It was just: smack, bam, you have MND and that's a deadly disease. Just like that.

No build-up, nothing. You are sick and you're gonna die. It could have been a little bit more subtle, don't you think?"

I nod. But I still don't say anything. What *can* I say? MND, yes, I heard about it. I know the posters, that once in a while appear all over the Netherlands. Photos of deceased people, who ask you to continue fighting the battle that they have lost. Very confronting, but at the same time: not really something that has been at the forefront of my mind. Because I don't know anyone who is suffering from MND.

Correction: I *didn't* know anyone who is suffering from MND.

But I do now.

"It's something to do with the muscles," he says, as we are trying to enjoy a cup of coffee at Atelier 84, a little cafeteria in Maaseik, Belgium, not far from his home. "But I don't know the details..."

A sip.

"...yet."

I look at him. For the first time since I met him, I don't know what to say.

"Just google it at home," he says. Then, full of self-confidence: "It's gonna be alright. Trust me."

"Do you really think so?" I ask.

"Yeah, why not? I mean: I feel quite good. It's just... It's just that bloody voice of mine. Makes it sounds worse than it actually is. It's starting to drive me up the wall."

Yes, that voice. The sound of a drunkard. I had noticed it as we were finishing *Fighting Spirit,* his highly acclaimed autobiography. All of a sudden, talking wasn't as easy as it should be anymore.

"Drives me fucking crazy," he continues. "Same for the swallowing. That's giving me trouble too. But apart from that, I don't feel sick. And remember: it's just an assumption. In a month's time I'll have a second opinion, at the medical university of Utrecht. Maybe they will draw a different conclusion."

He asks the waitress to bring him another bottle of mineral water. Then he wants to know what the situation is with the book presentation, five weeks from now at RKSV Minor in the tiny Dutch village of Nuth. Minor, *nomen est omen,* is the modest amateur side where the former professional started playing a few weeks ago, together with his brother Pedro.

"Fine," I say. "Mark van Bommel will receive the first copy."

"For free?"

"I think so."

"And how many books do I get? Not that I am going to read it. I'm not really, how shall I say it, an avid book reader. Besides, I already know the story and who's done it, hahaha!"

I smile.

"But it's always nice to have a few copies to give away, you know. Do you think I can get, let's say, twenty? Or wait, make that twenty-five. Winter's coming and my fireplace needs to be fed!"

This time he laughs even harder.

Typically Fernando, I think. No matter how dark the sky is, he always manages to so see the occasional ray of sun. That's a quality. A quality that I don't have. At least not now, at this very moment. I keep thinking about what Fernando has told me. About this deadly muscle disease. I want to know more about it. And I want to know that ASAP. I'm not going to wait until I'm home, that's for sure. So the moment Fernando has left the coffee joint to team up with Veronika and Isabella, who are shopping in a nearby street, I grab my phone. And I type that ominous abbreviation.

M

N

D

I immediately don't like what I read.

Motor Neurone Disease (MND) is an uncommon condition that affects the brain and nerves. It causes weakness that gets worse over time.

And, the part that really shocks me:

There is no cure, but there are treatments to help reduce the impact it has on your daily life. However, at this very moment, not a single patient has survived.

And there you have it. MND isn't a disease. It's a death sentence.

I start to swear, but not loud enough for the waitress to notice it.

As I leave the place, I remember what Fernando told me a few weeks ago. How he had trouble lighting a cigar. As if he didn't have enough strength to use a lighter.

It now makes sense.

A lot.

SEPTEMBER 27, 2013: **Fuss**

"About yesterday..." Fernando says, as I call him by phone, for a little chat. "First of all: super that this book presentation thing has been fixed now. And next week we're on *De Wereld Draait Door* (Holland's most popular talk show, hosted by a Dutch cross between Graham Norton and Jeremy Paxman with the haircut of one of the Nolan Sisters – ed.), that's really the icing on the cake. But hey, let's not talk about MND then. Let's wait. I don't want the whole nation to know it – as yet. Because it may just be a mistake. Maybe I don't have MND at all. Maybe the wrong information was in the wrong file. After all, that is a possibility! And what then? A lot of fuss about, well, nothing!"

"True," I answer. "Cos how are you now?"

"Fine, really. Happy to go training, later today. I feel great!"

"Good to hear that, man."

"Yeah. Playing football will always be the best thing in life."

"Got you 25 books, by the way."

"Okay. Let winter begin!"

OCTOBER 22, 2013: **Excesses**

Fighting Spirit, Fernando's autobiography, is not yer average football book. I know it, because I wrote it. Fernando knows it, because he lived it. But more and more media representatives are aware of it too. Because they read it . 'A book that gives you a shocking look into the destructive life of a former football player,' writes [free newspaper] *Sp!ts*. 'A life that reads like a book,' is the somewhat cryptic conclusion of weekly magazine *Panorama*. A local paper in Limburg, the province where Fernando was born, is the most outspoken of the lot. 'Shocking, honest, daring and full of fighting spirit!' it tells its readers. Very applicable, as the title of the book is, yep, *Fighting Spirit*. 'The former Fortuna, AZ, Glasgow Rangers and Zenit Saint Petersburg star tells all about his turbulent life.'

And turbulent it was indeed. Fernando himself once described it as wild water rafting. And more than once his boat hit the rocks. That's probably why he never made it as far as fellow footballers who had a smooth ride on a calm river.

Not that he never grabbed a prize, oh no. In fact, he won quite a lot. Three national titles, five national cups and two European trophies. Not bad, eh? On top of that he has been voted PFA Scotland Players' Player of the Year once, in 2005, which put him in the same league as, to name a few, Chris Sutton, Henrik Larsson, Paolo Di Canio, Charlie Nicholas and Paul Gascoigne.

But still, he could have reached so much higher, if it hadn't been for that unquenchable appetite for self-destruction. We once talked about it in his house in Maaseik, located along the busy road to Kinrooi. So you get the picture (or not).

"Some people say that thanks to your wild and excessive life style Michael Reiziger could take your place in the national team," I told him. "Because he was much more reliable, as a human being."

"Those people were probably right," he laughed.

“But that means you’ve missed out on at least fifty caps!”

“Right again. But hey, then I would have had sixty caps and not a nice life. And, more to the point, you wouldn’t have had a good book!”

So: no remorse. Not one single minute.

“But why is everyone constantly going on about my excesses? I needed to do all that shit! It took away the pressure. Do you have any idea about the immense pressure a professional footballer has to deal with? People really underestimate that. Just imagine, taking an important penalty kick while millions of people are watching you and millions of euros are at stake. You simply need to let some steam off, afterwards, to survive.”

“But you did enjoy it too,” I say.

“Of course! That’s why I have no regrets. No regrets at all.”

No regrets at all? Only a few. And that’s about the use of drugs, towards the end of his time in Russia. With that, he crossed a line – literally. It even lead to a suspension, after the Europa League clash with [Portuguese team] CD National, in 2009.

“I was depressed, at the time. I felt lonely. Not the best state to enter the VIP section of a trendy nightclub. Because there, behind the ropes, you find the real bad guys. Gangsters. Guys with coke to share. I didn’t have a starting position in the team. Didn’t have to play every week. That made me susceptible to snort the occasional line of Charlie. Until then, I’d always said no. But now I said yes, what the fuck. But I shouldn’t have done it. So yes, a few regrets after all.”

As I watch Fernando walking through the streets of sunny

Maaseik, together with Veronika and their 1,5 year old daughter Isabella, I can hardly believe that this is the same guy who once consumed truckloads of booze and babes. The wild guy from the book *Fighting Spirit*.

"I'm boring now, ain't I?" he laughs, as we sit down for lunch at Van Eyck, the majestic hotel in the heart of town, where we did so many interviews for the aforementioned book. "But who cares? I may be boring now, but I'm happy too. And that is what counts."

He pauses and points at Veronika, his stunning wife. He calls her 'Veronique', by the way. No idea why.

"I owe her so much," he says. "Without Veronique I wouldn't have been here today. I probably would have jumped from a balcony. Or at least I'd been a tramp in a Russian park, sipping vodka 24/7. I can tell you: Veronique saved my life."

"Do you remember what I said?" asks 'Veronique', who calls him 'Nando'. "Do you remember, Nando? I said to you: either you choose for a normal life with me, or..."

Or for a fucked up life without her. She doesn't have to finish the sentence.

"Yeah, I remember," he says. "I sometimes wish I'd met her fifteen years earlier. That would have been a hell of a lot better. But at least I have her now. Her and the little one."

"Any idea what Isabella will think of *Fighting Spirit*?" I dare to ask.

"I hope she reads it when she's 21," he chuckles.

"Do you think the book can warn her and other people?"

"Absolutely. And there's something else. It's better to have all of this shit printed already. You know why? Listen, my dream at the moment is to become coach of a really big professional football club. Imagine that in ten years from now, I will be head coach of Glasgow Rangers. What if then, all of a sudden, all kinds of stories about my drink and drugs use start to emerge? It's a lot better to come clean now, you know. Take the sting out already. And if they still want the juicy details, all I have to say is: read the book. It's probably still available at your local antiquarian, haha."

OCTOBER 27, 2013: **Rumours galore**

I receive an e-mail from journalist Ingrid Lemmens, who just had an interview with Fernando. She tells me that she got a bit suspicious, during her chat with the former footballer. Fernando had to go to the loo quite often. No, VERY often! "More and more people within Fortuna are confirming the fact that something serious is going on. That's why I mention it in my article. Out of respect for Fernando I did not dig too deep, during the interview. I have to tell you though, that more and more media are about to focus on it. That's why I'll write about it too. I hope you'll understand."

Yes, I do. After all, I'm a journalist myself. But I also understand that Fernando is not going to be amused, when I tell him about it. Which is exactly what happens. He is pissed off. And that doesn't change when I bring up the rumours that he may have cancer.

"Just leave it, will you? I'm still waiting for that phone call from the hospital. What if they apologise to me because they were wrong? I wouldn't be surprised if that happens. *Sorry Mr Ricksen, you don't have MND after all. You are perfectly healthy*. Which is exactly how I feel. Healthy. Apart from that fucked voice, that is. Hey, Vincent, you see it too, don't you? Don't I look healthy to you?"

OCTOBER 30, 2013: **De Wereld Draait Door**

"Hey Vincent, what time do we have to be in the studio for *De Wereld Draait Door*?"

"Around six, they said."

"Why six, for Christ's sake? Doesn't that show start at seven?"

"Yes, but we'll have to go through makeup first. And with a face like yours, that will take a while."

He sighs.

"Besides, we'll have to have a bite to eat too, right?

"I'm not hungry."

"C'mon, Fernando, just be there at six, as they request. We'll also have to have a quick chat with an editor, remember?"

As I put down the phone, I realise that I've never heard him being this insecure. He is obviously tensed. Something is going on. This is not the Fernando Ricksen who doesn't care about anyone or anything in the world.

He is on guard. And I know why.

Five weeks earlier, he had been on Dutch telly already. In a programme called *Bureau Sport,* he talked about his former addiction to alcohol. After the show had been broadcasted, he was slaughtered on social media. For the simple reason that everyone thought he was lying. Because of that voice. He was slurring his words. So he must have been drunk.

As we arrive at the studio, he still looks apprehensive. It's even worse than on the phone. Fernando is not at ease.

"You know..." he says, as we are climbing the stairs towards the editors' room, where [former Anderlecht and Ajax player-turned-novelist] Jan Mulder is drinking a cup of coffee, "...I think... I'm gonna say it."

I stop, two steps above him.

"You're gonna say WHAT?"

"The MND thing."

I'm surprised – to say the least.

"But... how about that all important second opinion you were talking about?"

"I don't care. At least people know I'm not pissed. Can't take that anymore. Can't handle the injustice. If I don't say it, people will still think I have been drinking. You know how much that has hurt me, after *Bureau Sport*? The truth is, I haven't had a drop of alcohol for months. I want people to know that my slurring hasn't got anything to do with booze. You know that's the truth, Vincent. Don't you?"

Fernando's sudden MND announcement causes a stir. It's less than an hour before the live programme starts, so it puts things upside down completely. But there is also commotion because at least one editor, Klaas Hazenoot, knows what the letters

MND stand for. This diagnosis means that Fernando Ricksen is going to die – soon.

Despite many years of experience in journalism, presenter Matthijs van Nieuwkerk is shocked when he is informed about the fact that the Ricksen item is not (just) going to be an animated conversation about the book.

"Are you sure you're gonna say it?" he asks.

"Yes."

"But can you handle it? I mean: emotionally?"

"Sure."

"I mean... We will talk about other things too. Katie Price and stuff. It's one gigantic leap from Katie to this. You don't mind?"

"No problem."

"Okay, well... Let's do it like this. I'm gonna talk about your book, ask you a few questions and then I want to know why you speak like this. And then you can reveal... Is that an idea?"

"Yep, fine."

I will be in the audience, but to be on the safe side I get a microphone pinned on me to. If all of a sudden Fernando can't say anything anymore, I'll have to take over. At least, that is the plan. But Fernando, very smartly dressed in a black shirt with a black tie, gives me a shoulder push. A soft one, nowhere near the ones he used to distribute when he was every opponent's nightmare. With the soft push he wants to say that there will be no need for me to take over. He, Fernando Ricksen, is going to answer all the questions. Just sit back, watch and be amazed, Mr De Vries!

On the way to the studio floor we meet [former speed skating champion] Erben Wennemars. When Fernando starts talking to him, he all of a sudden is his good old self again. Must be the adrenaline.

A few minutes later we are on air. As promised, Van Nieuwkerk grabs the book and reads what's on the autocue. "Booze, drugs and women – and then wasted. It happens quite often, in modern football. But seldom as much as with him. He was an exceptionally good defender. A huge talent, back in the Nineties. Twelve international caps. Enormous victories with Glasgow Rangers and Zenit Saint Petersburg. But on the other hand, there were always the devils called alcohol and sex. And in Russia they were joined by a third one: cocaine. All of this and more is featured in his autobiography *Vechtlust* (the original, Dutch title of *Fighting Spirit* – ed.)."

Van Nieuwkerk once again shows the book - a moment every single Dutch author is craving for, as *DWDD* is Holland's best watched talk show and when your book is featured on it, sales go sky high – and then turns to Fernando, who is sitting on his left.

"Fernando, it's almost as if you were eager to live two lives instead of one. The life of a good football player and the life of someone who can spend more money that he has ever dreamt of. A life full of girls, champagne and more girls. Did you manage to combine the two?"

Fernando nods. "I guess I did, yeah." And: "The excesses... didn't really affect... my career. I mean... I played for the.... Dutch national team. You can't... achieve that... by not... living as a... sports man. So yes... I think... I managed... to combine...

both lifestyles."

Left, right and centre of me I hear people laughing. At the same time Twitter is exploding. There's a drunkard on *DWDD*. Fernando has hit the bottle again. He is plastered. Without knowing what's really going on, total strangers chop off his head. Once an alcoholic, always an alcoholic.

It's just that it isn't true. I know he hasn't been drinking. I also know that this is the way he sounds now. Because of the illness he is probably suffering from. I all honesty: in all the months that we have been working on the book, I've never seen him drinking one glass of wine or one bottle of beer. Even when we went out to celebrate the finished product, he ordered mineral water.

But I am tensed. How will Fernando deal with what he is about to reveal in a few minutes, live on national television? How will he handle the fact that everyone will be aware of the fact that he thinks he is about to die? Can he control himself?

No, he can't.

First, we see a clip of Fernando, scoring against Ajax – with his heel. We see his red card against Roda JC – and the moment he makes his debut for the national team, as a substitute for [former Feyenoord and Manchester City star] Paul Bosvelt.

"You talk a bit slowly, at the moment," Van Nieuwkerk then says. "What's the story behind that?"

Fernando tries to answer the question. But he fails. His eyes are filled with tears.

He mumbles. "Month ago... Hospital... Seen... MND..."

He then turns his head towards me.

"Vincent..."

It's my turn. And I tell the viewers what Fernando just tried to say. That he has been diagnosed with MND. But also that he will go to hospital for a second opinion.

The audience shivers. Co-host Beau van Erven Dorens, sitting opposite Fernando, bends over and grabs his tattooed hand. "So good of you to be here, man," he says. "This is so brave of you. What a hero you are. It's so impressive that you didn't bottle out."

A big applause from the crowd. Van Nieuwkerk doesn't say anything anymore. Van Erven Dorens takes over and continues talking about the book.

"Was it good for you to tell your whole story?"

"Sure," is the answer. "It's a way of finishing a hectic period." He sounds a little more relaxed.

"Can I mention one name?" Van Nieuwkerk then interrupts.

Fernando smiles. He knows what's about to come.

"Katie Price. A bimbo, as the Brits say. Everybody there knows who she is. She's very popular. And very beautiful. Or, well, beautiful... Maybe 'juicy' is a better word. You write about her in the book in a chapter called Jackpot. Because she was the jackpot and you hit that jackpot. In other words: you managed to bed her."

"Or she managed to bed me," Fernando grins.

And there he is again: good old cheeky Fernando Ricksen. The audience laughs. Partly out of relief, probably. "Point taken, point taken!" yells Van Nieuwkerk. Then: "Did you enjoy your encounter with her?"

"It was great."

"I ask this, because you often hear that something like that is quite disappointing, when it actually happens."

"No, it was a top evening."

"You still remember the details?"

"Absolutely."

He then talks about the hookers who were lining up before and after matches of the Dutch national team and who ended up in many a player's room. This total lack of discipline was one of the reasons why Louis van Gaal quit as coach of the orange squad.

"But did you find true love, in the end?" Van Erven Dorens wants to know, seconds after Jan Mulder lied that 'those things' never happened in his time.

"Yes," says Fernando. And he mentions Veronika and Isabella.

"And are you loyal to her?"

"Yes. This is a new me. I am happier than ever."

Beautiful words, but Veronika doesn't hear them. She is in a hotel in Utrecht, the city where the next day Fernando will have his next set of medical examinations. There is a tv set on the room, but she decided not to watch. She couldn't handle it. "Nobody wants to see a loved one suffer."

That loved one leaves the tv studio immediately. He is too tired, too emotional to attend the traditional afterparty. Besides, he wants to go to bed early, to be in top shape the next day. The day of the check-up in Utrecht and the book presentation in Nuth. I agree with him: he should go. Right after I turned on my phone – 50 missed calls, 200 WhatsApp messages – I hug him and wish him all the best for tomorrow.

OCTOBER 31, 2013: **Book presentation**

It's around noon when he calls. "Bad news, Vincent."

And bad news it is. He suffers from ALS, Amyotrophic Lateral Sclerosis, AKA Motor Neuron Disease, MND. A deadly condition which kills one group of muscles after the other. Until you can't breathe anymore.

"And mine is even the most progressive form of all. So I will die fast."

"How fast?" I ask.

"Within four months."

I ask him how he feels. He says it's 'unreal'. "Yeah, I know my voice sounds funny. I also know that MND is a serious disease. VERY serious! It's just that… I mean, I feel fine, honest! I feel just like the man I was five months ago, Apart from the voice, nothing has changed."

He then tells me that his muscles ache. A lot. "Man, the needles that they put into them, to test the muscle action. So thick, so long… And they went in, so fucking deep… And everything without anaesthetics. You know I'm not a sissy, but this… Pfff. I can't remember having been in so much pain – EVER!"

I tell him that I fully understand him when he wants to cancel tonight's book presentation. But he rejects my proposal.

"You don't think I'm gonna let anybody taking this off me, do you? This is my little party. The more bunting the better. We worked long enough on this project. Got a pen?"

"One moment."

"Got it?"

"Yep."

"Write down: I am going to be the first person in the world to beat MND."

That evening he is going to repeat the phrase – into about ten different microphones. Because thanks to *De Wereld Draait Door*, the football canteen where the book presentation takes places is chock-a-block full. Eddy van der Ley, a well-known football journalist who acts as tonight's master of ceremonies, had said it already, earlier on in the week. "For a few hours, Nuth will be the centre of the world."

Pal Mark van Bommel, from PSV, AC Milan, Barcelona and Bayern Munich fame, tells me that Fernando's revelation on television, brought tears to his eyes. "I knew something was wrong. I just didn't know what that something was."

As much as he wasn't surprised that Fernando succeeded in shagging Katie 'Jordan' Price, Mark also doesn't find it strange that his former team mate is so strong, brave and confident regarding his current ordeal. "That's Fernando for you. I heard him saying that he is not going to give up. Of course he isn't. It's Fernando bloody Ricksen! This guy never gives up. Never!"

Mark is here to receive the first copy of Fernando's book, which he thinks is a big honour. "Besides that, I owe him something. As a youth player, I was kicked all over the pitch. But I never had to kick back. Because my friend Fernando did that for me. Mind you, I was pretty soft back then. Fernando taught me how to become a tougher player. And I am very grateful for that. Just image he hadn't been there. It's quite possible that I wouldn't have gotten any further than Fortuna Sittard!"

While Mark and Fernando hug each other like long lost friends – in reality the last time they've seen each other is just a few weeks ago – Veronika is flipping through the pages of her hubby's book. She's surprised it's as thick as it is. "Wow, 490 pages! Are people really gonna buy and read this?" she asks.

"Yes," I say to her. Of course I do. I would be a pretty lousy salesman if I'd say that it will gather dust forever – on the shelves of a discount shop. In fact, at that very moment, the first print is sold out already!

Part of the official presentation is an on stage interview with Eddy van der Ley. Of course Fernando's appearance in *De Wereld Draait Door* is part of the conversation. Just as the patient ordered. But not for too long, as this is meant to be a bit of a party. So next up are some more light hearted subjects. Ever-grinning Van der Ley is all too happy to bring up the subject of promiscuity. And for that, he turns to Mark van Bommel.

"Mark, according to Fernando you are the only person in football who isn't a love rat. Is that true?"

Mark knows how to entertain the crowd. "I've always wanted to be one," he says. "But every time I tried to grab a strange woman, Fernando was faster!

Laughter and applause.

"But on a more serious note: I was a very serious guy, that is true. So when Fernando went out hunting, I stayed in my room, because I wanted to sleep. Problem is: I shared that room with him. So every time he came back with a prey, I had to move out for a little while. In the middle of the night, yes."

More laughter.

"And you did that without hesitation", Van der Ley wants to know.

"Yes. I was out pretty fast."

Nuth goes nuts.

And that's even before Fernando recalls the evening he humped Katie Price. Or, more to the point, the evening Katie Price humped him. "It was a curry event for charity. She was the main guest. I remember our coach, Alex McLeish, telling us that absolutely nobody should try to pull her. But hey, before I knew she was on my lap. And what do you do then? Push her away? That would be very impolite! And stupid. Impossible too. The sexiest woman of Great Britain is pushing her groins onto my crotch. What do you think will happen?"

The term 'rise to the occasion' springs to mind.

"I am not made of stone, Eddy. So one thing lead to another. And in the end I was in bed with her."

"Something McLeish would have loved to happen to him," Van der Ley jokes.

"Absolutely. Because the next day at the training ground, with all of my team mates applauding, he said to me: 'Congratulations, you fucker. I don't know how you did it, but

I am very, very impressed. However, club regulations force me to give you a £ 25,000 penalty."

"Which you paid with a smile?"

"A big smile. It was a lot of money, but it was worth it. Every single penny."

After this and, er, some more funny moments, Fernando walks into the boardroom and kisses Veronika and Isabella. After that he gulps down a small bottle of Coke.

"Fantastic," he burps. "An evening like this, gives you so much energy. Positive energy, on top of that."

NOVEMBER 2, 2013: **Katie Price (1)**

"Heard about Katie Price?" I ask him.

"No. What about her? Did she pull another footballer?"

"No idea, but she is mad at you."

"Why? Because she's in my book?"

"She's pissed off. According to her, nothing happened between the two of you."

"Is that what she says?"

"Yeah, on Twitter. She does admit that you both had a great night, albeit one without sex."

"Do you really think I will make up a thing like that?"

"She did describe you as 'a beautiful man', by the way."

"And that isn't a lie either."

NOVEMBER 18, 2013: **Mixed feelings**

I meet Fernando in Maaseik, to talk with him about the previous, very emotional weeks. Once again we do that in the Van Eyk Hotel. According to the guest book, Formula One racing driver Max Verstappen has been here too. As well as Kim Holland, the country's most notorious porn actress.

"Were they together?" laughs Fernando.

Nice to see him in good spirit again.

"Man..." he starts, as we sit down. "It's like the whole world has seen me on *De Wereld Draait Door*. I remember I went to the super market, a few days later. I needed a carton of milk..."

"...and you came back four hours later," says Veronika.

"Yeah, Veronique was getting worried already. But it was surreal. Complete strangers wanted to talk to me, one after the other!"

"How do you look back at the show yourself?" I ask Fernando.

"With mixed feelings," he answers. "Of course, I am glad that I told it. That was a relief. But the fact that I cried on telly... I mean, it's not something that I like doing. But I couldn't help it. It's the emotions. When I get emotional, it's lockjaw time. Not nice, but it's the way it is."

"Presenter Van Nieuwkerk couldn't say much either."

"Yeah, I noticed that. So it's good that there was a co-host, Beau. He lost a friend to MND, so he knew exactly how to handle. It was the right tone of voice."

"And you, Veronika? How do you feel?"

"Shit," she says. "After all the troubles with drink and drugs and women and violence, I finally thought he was entering a quiet period. We just started a new life. Our life, together with Bella. And then this..."

I don't say anything, as Veronika starts sobbing.

"All our plans for the future... gone!"

I still don't say a word.

"At first I hoped that it was cancer. Although that is a very strange way of putting it. You don't ask for cancer, never! But then at least Nando would have been able to speak and move and... You know, there isn't even a cure for MND!"

But Veronika, whose father committed suicide when she was seven, hasn't lost all hope yet. And that is because Fernando's fighting spirit allows him to still act like not much is happening. That damn voice, yes, but the rest of him is still okay. Or so it seems.

"I'm still capable of doing basically everything," says Fernando. "I walk, I drive my car, I do groceries..."

It's just that voice, that turned to be a real obstacle. It's the reason why he stopped training Fortuna's youth. "I can't immediately tell the kids what I want to tell them. It takes ages until the words leave my lips. And that's very ineffective. Hence my decision to stop."

"But when I see him playing with Bella," adds Veronika, "it's a completely different story. What I see then, is by far not a sick man. I see a happy man, without any worries. Yes, that sounds strange, but it's true. And you know what? At such times I really, really realise that Nando is the love of my life. But..."

She starts smiling.

"...it wasn't exactly love at first sight. Mind you, I wasn't looking for love at all, when I first met him in Saint Petersburg, way back in 2007. But the guy kept calling me. So one day I said to myself: whatever, let's just do it. And we went on a date. Which turned out to be quite nice. So after that we did it again. And again."

And, as Fernando makes his way to the bathroom: "He didn't speak Russian, I didn't speak English. You can say that those nights were kinda, unusual, haha. He later taught me English. Yeah, thanks to him I can speak the language. He really wanted the best for me. Wanted to take me further in life. I immediately noticed that he was very social, despite all the rumours around him. He really has a very sweet character. Just look at Bella. She's really Daddy's girl. You have no idea how often she kisses his photo..."

A breath of air. Then: "He was one of football's hard men. But that was then and this is now."

"He wasn't just hard, he was mean too," I say.

"Yes, but he is completely different as a father. I think he is one of the nicest fathers in the entire universe. And that's since the day she was born. Nando's current illness has got nothing to do with it. Sometimes he is even a bit *too* sweet. Like last week, when Nando was eating chocolate in front of the telly. Bella came to him and asked for a piece too. And he gave it to her, just like that. Although chocolate isn't good for her. But Nando didn't care. My little girl likes chocolate, so Daddy gives her chocolate. Because Daddy loves her. What can I say then?"

Fernando, back from having a leak: "I try to fit MND into my life. But it's difficult, because I don't really have the symptoms – yet. I can still move my arms. I can still breathe properly. Yes, I know what's about to come. It's getting worse and worse and worse. Eventually I will become a wreck. That's what MND is about. But it's so difficult to picture myself like that, because right now, I can still do pretty much everything!"

Veronika: "And that's why we still live our life as if nothing has happened. It's useless to adapt to a situation that hasn't occurred as yet. So we still go on holiday and we still take Bella to the zoo. Notwithstanding the verdict, we are a totally normal little family."

"Death's behind me," says Fernando. "That's why I try to look forwards."

"That's why we don't put too much emphasis on the illness," adds Veronika. "For example: we are not filming 24/7, just to have as much footage of our family as possible, for when Fernando… You know? Filming every little thing would feel very forced. Not natural."

I want to know if they are afraid of the future.

"No," says Fernando. "I know my days are numbered. But I don't kinda accept that. There is simply too much that I still want to do. I want to see Bella growing up. That's something to fight for. So I will fight. Like I've always done."

"And we still want to get married," says Veronika. "So I hope the divorce (from Graciela – ed.) will be made official very soon. If that's the case, we'll tie the knot. Here and in Russia."

Fernando and Veronika still have a bond with the latter. Hence the fact that they raise Isabella in three languages:

Dutch, English and Russian.

"Nando already bought the wedding ring," whispers Veronika. "I hope I can put it on my finger very soon. I really love this man. Can't think of a life without him. *Won't* think about a life without him. Not yet. We're still too happy to do that."

NOVEMBER 22, 2013: **Exhausted (1)**

"Rumour has it that Fernando fucked every single woman in Sittard. Does that include the two of you?"

Bram Endedijk is a reporter for Powned, Holland's most notorious and scandalous broadcasting company. This is the kind of questions he has to ask. And the two blonde ones who went to the Fortuna Sittard stadium to have their copy of *Fighting Spirit* signed, don't even feel offended.

"Of course he did us too!" says Blondie number 1.

"You don't really think he skipped us, do you?" says Blondie number 2.

Half an hour later, Endedijk knows that not just Fernando and the two blondes, but practically the whole town of Sittard is mental. It's after he heard of the antics of formal football thug John Linford (Ipswich Town, Colchester United, Southend United, Birmingham City and many other clubs), who used to drop his trousers, every time he was in a pub in Sittard, and whack his todger on the counter. That's why they called him *The Elephant Man*. Needless to say that Endedijk now wants to do an item in Sittard every single week.

"Unbelievable," sighs Fernando, looking at the enormous amount of people lining up for his autograph.

I watch him signing one book after the other. And I notice the fact that he doesn't hold the pen like he used to do. Like everybody does. In fact, his thumb is twisted around the writing tool, like a stripper around a pole. I ask him if this is the first symptom of MND, or if he is just tired. Because he *looks* tired. Barely thirty minutes of signing and there are bags under his eyes the size of Mick Jagger's lips. But he doesn't want to stop the session. Because he doesn't want to disappoint anybody.

But at a certain moment he has to stop, as tonight's match against FC Dordrecht is about to begin. Still, he tells the crowd that he will be back in two weeks time. So every single fan with an as yet unsigned book, will have a second chance in fourteen days time.

Typically Fernando. No unfinished business for him.

NOVEMBER 28, 2013: **A twist of fate**

Fernando is going on tour. Thanks to Eddy van der Ley, who arranged a string of Q&A evenings with, believe it or not, a Fernando Ricksen Quiz. The schedule mentions dates in Panningen, Heerlerheide, Glasgow, East Kilbride, Wishaw and Ayr.

But we start the *Fernando Ricksen Experience Tour* in Hengelo, a rather big town in the east of the Netherlands, close to the border with Germany. Fernando will be joined by his former Rangers team mate Bert Konterman.

I meet the main man on the parking lot of the venue where the Ricksen event is to be held. He looks smart, in his turtleneck sweater with – gulp! – skulls. And relieved. Relieved that he didn't catch a cold, last week at the windy and rainy Fortuna v Dordrecht game. Catching a cold isn't something you want to happen, in his situation. Imagine him getting pneumonia. That would be quite dangerous.

"How many men inside?" he wants to know.

"About 200," says Van der Ley, who then tells Fernando what the plan is. "First I announce Bert, then you, Fernando. And remember: tonight is about fun! We're gonna have a ball. Got it?"

Fernando nods.

And then the car dealer, on whose premises the event is about to take place, steps forward. "What kind of music do you want to hear?"

Fernando smiles and says: "I don't care. Just play what you have."

"*Fernando* by ABBA?"

"Whatever."

"It hurts."

Fernando grabs his jaw and looks at Remco Regterschot, a sports journalist who wants to know how he feels. "Eating has become more difficult. Speaking too. It's so weird. I mean, a year ago nothing was wrong with me!"

He shakes his head. "I think it's just bad luck, man. Very bad luck. This could have happened to anyone. And as you can see, it even happens to people who have always been top fit."

"Why are you here tonight?" the interviewer wants to know.

"I wanted a bit of distraction," is the honest answer.

"And how are you dealing with the situation, at the moment?"

"In a way I am glad that at least I know *what* is wrong with me. It's better than the uncertainties. But having said that... It's a tough one, this ordeal. It's a burden. Nothing less than that."

"You said: one day, someone will beat this disease. Let me be that someone."

"Exactly. Someone has to be the first one. Look, one day there will be a medicine. But when? Right now, MND is just a slow lane towards death. Simply because that all important medicine doesn't exist yet."

"Does that make you angry?"

"No. Who do I have to be angry with? It's the way it is."

"You're a famous person. Do you feel you could become some kind of ambassador in the battle against MND?"

"Maybe. So far, very few people had heard about MND. Maybe now, because I have it, more people will become aware of it. It is a possibility. Anyway, whatever happens, I will try to keep smiling for as long as I can. Because being positive works better than being negative. Did you read my book, by the way?"

"Of course I did."

"And?"

"You're fucking insane."

"I *was*, haha. But at least I've lived."

"No doubt about that, Fernando."

"Look, there's good old Bert Konterman. Do you know the nickname he had, in Glasgow? *Master of Disaster*. Would have been more appropriate for me, don't you think? Haha."

Of course it would. After all, Konterman has always been a devoted Christian. If both of them had been on your shoulders, as you sometimes see on a cartoon, Konterman would have been the angel and Ricksen the devil.

"One day Arthur Numan and I were visiting Fernando in Saint Petersburg," says Konterman, as part of the Q&A with presenter Eddy van der Ley. "It's just that he never showed up. He'd had an away game in Moscow and simply didn't return to Saint Petersburg afterwards. He stayed in Moscow for 36 long hours. Hours filled with drinking, snorting and shagging. At least, that's what I read in the book. At the time, Arthur and I didn't have a clue."

"Strip joints," says Van der Ley, acting as if he's never been to one. "What's so good about them?"

"The whole package," answers Fernando.

Impressive stories, but not quite as impressive as what's happening after the interview, when Fernando staggers towards a fellow MND patient who is in a wheelchair already. He puts his arm around her and stays like that, while time seems to freeze. They hold each other, they chat and the onlookers hold their breath. Two MND patients, at different stages of the disease.

No need for words anymore.

NOVEMBER 29, 2013: **Wheelchair**

"So good what you did yesterday," I tell him. "With that woman in the wheelchair."

"Why? Just a little effort."

"But still... You did it."

"Yes."

"Do you ever think: one day it will be me, in that wheelchair?"

"No. I refuse to think that much ahead. All I know is that I quit once I'm not able to wipe my own bum anymore."

DECEMBER 13, 2013: **The Louden Tavern**

Of course, Fernando's revelation about his health didn't just cause a stir in his native country, but also in Scotland. After all, he was (and is) very much loved there. Needless to say the British press couldn't stop writing about it. For five (!) days in a row, Fernando made the front and back pages of the *Scottish Sun*. With headlines so heavy they would crash your skull if they fell on you. And hey, this wasn't about World War III. No, it was just the antics of a former Glasgow Rangers footballer who once shagged Katie Price, snorted coke (more than once), had several fights with Paul Le Guen, was threatened with death by the IRA and indulged in drunken orgies with girls who didn't even introduce themselves other than giving blowjobs left, right and, of course, centre.

The fans loved it.

Of course they did!

Hence the initiative from Robert Marshall, who owns [Rangers pub] The Louden Tavern on Copland Road in Glasgow, to invite Fernando for a Q&A. "I want to let him know that we, Rangers fans, haven't forgotten about him. But I fully understand it if he can't make it, given the current circumstances."

Can't make it?

This is Fernando Ricksen we're talking about. Fernando, the ultimate Fighting Spirit! So off he goes to Glasgow, for not one, but two sold-out evenings with the Rangers family.

"Last time I was in Scotland must have been 2006," he says, as we meet each other at Amsterdam's international airport Schiphol.

"That must have been as a Zenit player," I answer. "In a game *against* Rangers."

"Man, what a game it was..."

"Didn't go smoothly, did it?"

"I told Chris Burke, who just got back from an injury, not to dribble. And what did he do?"

"He dribbled."

"Exactly. Non stop. Drove me insane."

"So you kicked him."

"Sort of."

"Sort of?"

"I kicked the ball. And, er, his ankle. And off poor Burke went, straight to the dressing room. With yet another injury."

"Ouch."

"Yeah, you can say that. Man, they hated me, in that stadium.

The Rangers crowd hated me. Their whistles hit me like whip cracks."

But that was then and this is now.

"So glad you're back!" says the first Scotsman we meet in the lobby of the Thistle Hotel on Cambridge Street. He even kisses him. On the cheek, thank God.

"I'm as glad as you are," says Fernando, trying to escape from two tattooed hands the size of ship's propellers.

As we do the check-in, I ask Fernando if he first wants to take a nap, before we hit the town and face 500 crazy supporters.

"No thanks. I prefer to show you the city. Ever been here? Man, I'm dying to see what has changed, since I've lived here. Maybe I can show you my former house."

"Newton Mearns."

"No, not that one. The one in Glasgow itself. Newton Mearns was shit. Full of stuck-up bastards. Fuck, I hated it!"

So that's what we'll do. We're gonna paint the town, er, blue. After a quick lunch at the hotel restaurant. A greasy club sandwich. Well, what do you expect? For delicious food, Fernando should have played in Barcelona or Naples. Not in, with all respect, Glasgow. Insert your own fried Mars bar comment here.

So off we go, by taxi. Past the Kelvingrove Art Gallery and Museum in Argyle Street. But, more important, past [Indian restaurant] Mister Singh's and [strip club] Seventh Heaven. In Sauchiehall Street, the pubs are filled already.

Fernando knows Seventh Heaven by heart. He has also

been a regular at Mister Singh's. But he's never been to the Kelvingrove. He's hardly been inside a museum full stop. Yes, he visited the world famous Hermitage in Saint Petersburg, for four long minutes. "That was enough. I'm simply too restless to stand still and stare at a painting. Can't focus. Which in a way is strange, as I never had problems focusing on an opponent."

We turn into Byres Road, where Glasgow University is. Not that Fernando... Well, you get the picture.

"I hated school, as a kid. Couldn't wait to leave and play for the Fortuna youth. But a university like this one... I wouldn't have minded being a student here."

"Yeah, because of the girls!" cheeky Van der Ley shouts from the back seat.

"Among other things," says Fernando, dead serious. "I really think I could have studied here. A language or so. I mean: you all know how fast I've been in learning English."

As we approach the Kelvinside Paris Church Òran Mór, a pub now, Fernando starts talking about Jimmy Bell, Rangers' legendary kit man. "Good old Jimmy. First Scot I met here. Top guy. But you couldn't understand what he said. That fucking accent... Even when I was drunk, I didn't recognize the words!"

"That's Scotland for you," says Van der Ley. "Same goes for the stuff they're wearing. I remember a photo of you in one of those bloody kilts."

"Must have been 2005, when I was voted Player of the Year. It was a blue one."

"And? Did you go commando?"

"No way. The thing was made of sheep wool. Way too itchy!

Would have ended up scratching my balls, during the ceremony. Not very classy. Hence the jocks."

No pun intended here!

We then talk about the weather in Scotland. Nearly every day, BBC weather woman Judith Ralston, the one with the heavy glasses and even heavier boobs, has to announce yet another day of rain.

"I hated it in the beginning," he says. "But after a while you get used to it. And as from a certain moment I couldn't care about all that cold water anymore. You learn how to deal with it. After all, it's a tough men's game. Oh wait, that's Squinty Bridge and there, at Lancefield Quay, do you see those apartments? I used to live there, top floor. You see the balcony? Oh man, this may have been the best place I've ever lived! So much to do in the neighbourhood. And we're not just talking about restaurants, if you know what I mean..."

Big wink.

"Do you see the hotel, over there? That's the one. That's where Katie Price and I... Well, you know the story."

Of course we do. Everyone does. But we still like the tale. Hence the first question at that evening's event at The Louden. It's not about a goal, or a free kick or a red card. It's about a busty babe. THAT busty babe. It's what the crowd wants to know: how did Fernando manage to play hide the sausage with the nation's number 1 sex symbol?

I look at Fernando and can hardly believe my eyes and ears. These people LOVE him. The cheering, it's almost ear-splitting.

It's almost as if Jesus Himself has returned. But Jesus didn't have porcelain teeth. At least, not that we know.

He loves the attention. And, unlike in the television studio, he keeps his emotions under control. He smiles. These are his people – and he knows it.

Somebody throws a red, white and blue scarf at him. He grabs it in a reflex. Just like that. As if nothing is wrong with his motor function.

Many pints of lager later – this lot know how to drink! – Van der Ley asks if somebody has 'one last question'.

"Yes!" screams a guy with a face like a currant bun.

I wonder what he would like to ask. Are there any questions left? I mean: I think I've heard them all.

"Fernando, who is your favourite player?"

"Fernando, how does it feel to be back?"

"Fernando, who was your favourite team mate?"

"Fernando, what are your thoughts about Dick Advocaat?"

"Fernando, what was your best ever game?"

He answered every single question. So by now they must know basically everything about him.

They know that he is a big fan of Lionel Messi.

They know that he thinks it's great to be back.

They know that Barry Ferguson and Arthur Numan were his favourite team mates.

They know that Dick Advocaat is the best coach he's ever had.

They know that The Old Firm of January 9, 2005, in which he scored with a magnific header, is the best game he ever played for Rangers.

So what's left to know?

"Fernando, what's your favourite car?"

No, I didn't see that one coming either.

Is this guy taking the piss? Is he pissed himself? No he isn't. He is dead serious. And so is Fernando, as he answers the spotted one's question.

"A bright red Ferrari 550 Maranello. But not once it's total-loss after one's ex has used it."

Because that is what happened. He bought the car from his big friend Colin McRae. And then his wife wrecked it. "And then they get furious when you say that women can't drive."

"THIS WAS A-MA-ZING!!" yells Marshall. "NOW WE KNOW EVERYTHING ABOUT FERNANDO!!"

Yeah, everything but the answer to that most important question. "Fernando, how much time do you have left?" He doesn't know it. Nobody does. That's MND for you, one of the most unpredictable diseases in the history of mankind.

As we return to the hotel, Fernando reveals that he's had a top night.

"Wanna go for a drink?" Van der Ley asks him.

"Better not," is the answer. "I am tired. And I have to be in good shape by tomorrow."

"You're getting old," I tease him.

"True. Just imagine: in the good old days I went out at this time. And now I just want to sleep. Things are not what they used to be."

I give him a hug and thank him for the nice evening. As he pushes the button of the elevator, I notice that his fingers are more crooked than before.

DECEMBER 26, 2013: **Straight from the heart**

Boxing Day. I sit in front of the telly and watch *Recht uit het hart* (Straight from the heart), a programme by [catholic broadcasting company] KRO in which selected people tell about the highs and, especially, lows in their lives. On it tonight is Fernando. In front of a live audience he reads aloud, without stammering even once.

"Like every other boy, I had just one big dream: to become a professional football player. And not just that. I wanted to become the best professional football player. The best from the Netherlands. The best from Europe. The best from the entire world. I remember playing in the streets of my hometown, every single day. Playing until dark. Until the street lights went on. And, ultimately, until I reached the top.

I did reach the top. Via Fortuna Sittard and AZ I ended up at Glasgow Rangers, one of the biggest clubs in the world. After that I signed for Zenit Saint Petersburg, in Russia. With every single club we became champions. That, in itself, is unique. In Scotland I even won more than one title – as the team captain, on top of that. With Zenit we became champions of Europe. I also played for the national team. Twelve times, to be precise. I had reached the top – just like I've always wanted, as a kid. My dream wasn't a dream anymore. It was reality.

But there was a downside to my success story. The attention, the pressure, the money, the wealth, the women, I couldn't deal with it. Not in a normal way. At first, I thought acting like a clown would take the pressure off. So I came up with lots of pranks. I set off fireworks, in the middle of Summer. I threw our chairman into the pool. The poor guy couldn't even swim. I fought with whoever was getting on my nerves. And I started drinking. Lots. Until I got addicted.

I was an alcoholic.

After numerous incidents, I went into rehab, at a clinic near London. I didn't have a choice: it was do or die. It was the first time that I realised what a mess my life had become. It was total chaos. Glasgow Rangers didn't want me anymore – and neither did my wife. I simply had to clean up.

And I did.

Four weeks inside made me a different human being. Less selfish. I was reborn, so to say.

But it didn't take long before things turned bad again. Worse than before, even. More extreme.

Back in Russia I got hooked on booze again. But this time I went dealing with another demon too.

Cocaine.

People sometimes ask me: do you have any regrets? The answer is: hardly. I only regret that I started doing drugs. It caused a terribly long suspension. It made me depressed. I almost got suicidal tendencies. No, I never stood on a bridge, wanting to jump. But I came close.

It's just that I had a fantastic girlfriend, Veronika. And thank God I still have her. She became the mother of our wonderful little baby, Isabella. Without Veronika I couldn't have made it. Without Veronika I wouldn't have been here today.

For me, there's only one goal in life left. I want to get old with Veronika and Isabella. I want to lead my life with those two. A new, completely different life from the one I had. And it seemed to work. I'd quit professional football. I'd put my turbulent past in a book. I was ready for the future. Our future.

But it all went wrong. I got MND, that most feared disease. And now my future is uncertain. And most certainly it doesn't stretch as far as I wanted.

But I don't give up. I never did. Not as a footballer, not as a human. One day, somebody will be able to beat MND. Somebody will be the first. Let me be that somebody."

I look at it, I listen and I think: you're a very, very brave man, Fernando...

2014:
The Acceptance

JANUARY 11, 2014: **Applause**

We're back in Glasgow. Not for the umpteenth Q&A, but for a visit to Ibrox, the temple where in the past, high priest Fernando showed many a piece of silverwork to his devoted followers.

A lot has changed, since those halcyon days.

And not just with Fernando.

Glasgow Rangers went into administration thanks to a tax debt of about 9 million pounds. They were expelled from the Premier League to end up in a division with clubs like Peterhead, Montrose and East Stirlingshire.

A humiliation.

They weren't even allowed/able to keep their name. Glasgow Rangers became Rangers. Well, that could have been worse. Gaelic Rangers or so.

Just joking!

Fernando is furious, when we talk about what happened to his beloved club. "The other clubs could have prevented it," he fumes. "But apart from Kilmarnock they all voted against us staying on the highest level. It's a bloody shame! But hey, they don't know Rangers then! This is one club you don't fuck with! Rangers will always come back. Rangers will never die. Not with the support we have. The big Rangers family is loyal as hell. So it's just a matter of time before we are back where we belong. And from then on, we will stay there!"

It's obvious, Fernando still has a red, white & blue soul.

Anyway, today the once mighty Rangers have to face East Fife, one of the two clubs that make up the most-told joke in the history of football ("And now today's results: East Fife four, Forfar five."). It's been eight long years since Fernando visited Ibrox for the last time. He has heard that he will be officially honoured today, as a very special guest. "Typically Rangers," he says. "They really know how to deal with ex-players. They will never forget you."

"Not just Rangers," adds Veronika. "Russian clubs are just as thoughtful."

"I know," says Fernando. "Ask Dick Advocaat. He was driven around the stadium in a Bentley. Not once, but twice."

"Do you think you're gonna cry today?" I ask him.

"Don't know."

"What's gonna be the most difficult bit, you think?"

"Knowing that it's probably the last time I will ever set foot on that turf."

He stares, nowhere in particular.

"You know what they're gonna play when the teams walk onto the grass, right?"

I do. "It's *Simply the Best* by Tina Turner, right?"

"It sure is. Dick's idea (which, in all honesty, he must have borrowed from PSV Eindhoven – ed.). He wanted a song that made us feel invincible. And invincible we became. We won basically everything. Thanks to that song."

"And to a pretty good squad, I would say!"

"Oh yes. Most definitely. All those magnificent Dutchmen. Michael Mols, Arthur Numan, Giovanni van Bronckhorst,

Ronald de Boer... But there was more. Jean-Alain Boumsong, the Frenchman. And what about Craig Moore and Barry Ferguson? Believe me: you wouldn't want to have those two as opponents!"

"Same goes for a certain Fernando Ricksen."

"The guy who never gave up? Yeah, that's why they loved me so much. But I didn't do it just for them, not to put on a show. It came natural. I've always been a fighter. Well, you know that, as you wrote the book."

He smiles.

"But it's really fantastic to know that they haven't forgotten about me, at Ibrox. Talking about that: we mustn't forget to ask the cab driver to drop us off right at the entrance. By no means earlier!"

As we enter the stadium, I realise why he requested to be driven to the front door of Ibrox. It's the crowd. If he had been asked to leave the taxi at one of the roundabouts near the stadium, he wouldn't have been able to make it in time. The mass would have eaten him alive – in a nice way.

So off to the main entrance it is. There, Carol Patton (Rangers' press manager since the invention of sliced bread), welcomes Fernando by putting her hand on his shoulder. For a few years she has been his confidential counsellor at the club – and she loves welcoming him back. "Sooo glad to see you!"

It was Carol's idea to invite him for today's, er, clash with East Fife. So the club could honour him at halftime.

"Oh, by the way," she says, as we walk through the intestines of the majestic stadium, "can you do the raffle too?"

"That what?"

"The raffle."

"That means..."

"...that we ask you to pull the prize winning tickets."

"No problem. No problem at all. But I would like to say something to the fans too, if I can."

"Of course you can. What is it that you want to say, Fernando?"

"I would like to thank them for their eternal support. It really means a lot to me."

As we walk a bit further, we bump into a young woman named Rebecca Mennie. She confesses to Fernando that his photo was on the wall of her teenager's room. She also tells him that she raised 200 pounds for MND Scotland, which she likes to hand over to Fernando, symbolically. "And there's more to come," she tells him. I'm gonna do a sponsor run as well. Half a marathon. Hope I can finish it, as I am not really an athlete. But I'll give it a try."

He hugs her, a bit clumsy.

"And there is something I would like to ask you," she then says.

"Go ahead."

"Can I have my picture taken with you?"

We'll watch the game from the Director's Box, not far from the Rangers dug-out. This time, Ally McCoist starts with guys like Cammy Bell, Sébastien Faure, Lee McCulloch, Fraser Aird, Lee Wallace, Nicky Law, Andrew Little and Jon Daly. Plus Dean Shiels, from Northern Ireland, who previously played for Hibernian, Doncaster Rovers and Kilmarnock. "A good one," says Fernando. And within five minutes, 'the good one' scores. 1-0 to Rangers. The crowd explodes.

"That was a brilliant goal!" I scream at Fernando. "What a volley!"

"Yeah, that wasn't too bad."

"You never made 'em like that, did you?"

He looks at me and says: "Remember the free kick against Aberdeen? If not, check it on YouTube."

As the end of the first half is approaching, Fernando, Veronika, Isabella and Carol are waiting for the referee's halftime whistle. He looks cool, thumbs up, self-confident, ready to make his way onto the pitch. As the 22 players dive into their respective dressing rooms, for their well-earned cup of tea, the speaker announces today's special guest. And as he does that, I can see the sudden change on Fernando's face. The lips start trembling and the eyes get watery.

And there he goes, in his heavy winter coat with fur collar. As the stadium erupts, so do Fernando's lacrimal glands. He waves at the crowd, applauds, sniffs... And as he reaches the centre spot of the green carpet, he loses it. The former hard man of Scottish football cries, like many of his opponents did in the past. The speaker asks him to grab the prize winning tickets, but Fernando has trouble accomplishing this easy task. I see his crooked fingers and realise: this is what suffering looks like.

It's heartbreaking.

'FERNANDO STAY STRONG', reads a banner on one side of the stadium. He raises his hands to give his devotees a big thank you. But he can hardly stretch his arms.

Heartbreaking indeed.

Two minutes later, he is back in the belly of Ibrox, where he falls into Veronika's arms. Crying. Empty. Completely empty.

He wants to go.

As he stumbles into the hotel lobby, Shiels scores the 2-0.

JANUARY 12, 2014: **Ally McCoist**

I want to know what went wrong yesterday, all of a sudden.

"Locked again, er?"

"Yep. Immediately. It's that damned compulsive crying. When it comes, it comes. You can't stop it."

"It's okay. Nobody will blame you for it."

"It's fucked, Vincent. I'm not ashamed of it, it's just… Did you see what a stupid face I pulled? C'mon man, I'm one ugly fucker when that happens! Drooping mouth and eyelids. Gosh, what a face! Anyway, was it any good after I left?"

"Yeah. I met Ally McCoist."

"Good guy. Great he's their manager."

"I had my picture taken with him."

"Super. Did he say anything to you?"

"He introduced me as Rangers' latest signing."

"Haha."

"He hopes you'll be back soon."

"No problem. I love Rangers."

"But hey, how are you now?"

"Think as from now on, I'm gonna slow things down."

"Really?"
"Just kidding."

FEBRUARY 1, 2014: **The first cracks**

No Fernando, all day. No text message, no call, nothing.

A few minutes after 2 PM I hear why. He doesn't feel well.

In fact, he feels so weak that he can't make it to the venue in Heerlerheide. Bad timing, as his lecture was meant to begin at this very moment. So we'll have to cancel it.

As Eddy van der Ley tells the audience that Fernando just reported sick, I recall the occurrences in Panningen from two weeks ago. It was another day without a single sign of life. But at least he showed up, at the very last moment. But it wasn't the same anymore. It wasn't the one who did the raffle at Ibrox. He had a funny walk. Not one to laugh about, oh no. It was sad to see. He walked like an old man.

"That's MND for you," says Sanne van Haandel, who was really hoping to see Fernando this afternoon. Not for herself, but for the person in the wheelchair in front of her. That person is Michele Turnu, a former bodybuilder, who suffers from MND himself. Sanne is his personal nurse.

"It started with a clog foot," Michele says. "But after some medical examination at the hospital in Nijmegen it turned out to be MND."

"And that while he's always lived healthy," Sanne says. "He

never ate shit food. He always trained. And still... I mean: we're talking about a former Benelux (Belgium/Netherlands/ Luxemburg – ed.) champion!"

She tells how Michele at first refused to use a wheelchair. Until he simply *had* to.

At least his speech is unaffected, unlike Fernando's. So we can clearly hear him when he says that he's not going to give up.

"Just like Fernando always says," I add.

"Exactly. And later this month we go to Colombia. For stem cell therapy. I will try everything to beat – or at least slow down – the disease."

I tell him that Fernando wants to go to Israel, for exactly the same treatment.

Sanne then asks if I will ask Fernando if he wants to meet them some other time, when he's feeling better. I promise to do that.

As they make their way out, I start calculating. It's been four months since Fernando's diagnosis. And now he's already too bad to show up at an event. I freeze.

Four months...

Maybe the doctors were right after all.

APRIL 24, 2014: **Sandy Jardine**

Sad news from Scotland. Sandy Jardine passed away.

The Rangers legend, who played no less than 451 official games for Glasgow Rangers, lost his battle against cancer. He fought like the red lion in the club crest, but succumbed to the illness at 65. Like Fernando, he was a fighter. It's just that he had to face a dishonest opponent. Just like Fernando.

"Do you ever realise that one day you may lose the fight too?" I ask him.

"Of course I do. But at the same time: look what happened to Paul Walker."

"The actor from the *Fast & Furious* movies?"

"Yes, that one. Hit a tree and got killed. You never know what's going to happen. Never."

MAY 15, 2014: **Corona**

"Just don't tell anyone I support Celtic," the man next to me whispers with a smile.

We are in Glasgow again, Fernando and me, and this time we are accompanied by Michiel Blijboom, who wrote the English version of Fernando's book, which will be presented tomorrow. Tonight, we are having a pre-book launch dinner at Mister Singh's, the Indian restaurant at Elderslie Street, where the Indian waiters – Blijboom calls them McTikka and McPapadum - walk around in kilts. Fernando is wearing a T-shirt with a big print of a skull.

Before he has a look at the menu, the translator wants to see the photo of Sean Connery, one of the restaurant's more famous guests. After that, we sit down and order our drinks. Fernando wants a cola, but because of his current problems with articulating, he's been given a Corona.

In other words: beer.

Alcohol.

"Just a few sips," he says, as he grabs the glass with the basal joints of his thumbs.

"Did you notice that?" Blijboom asks me, as Fernando makes his way to the loo. "He drinks with both hands, like children do. Poor bastard."

MAY 21, 2014: **Testimonial (1)**

We are at the stadium of Fortuna Sittard, where we announce the line-up for Fernando's first ever testimonial. More precisely: the line-up of the team called Fernando's All Stars. They will face the current Fortuna squad.

Meet the All Stars:

Ronald Waterreus

Oscar Moens

Kevin Hofland

Giovanni van Bronckhorst

Rick Geenen

Gino Facenna

Ivica Krizanac

Michael Reiziger

Wilfred Bouma

Pedro Ricksen

Szabolcs Huszti

Mark van Bommel
Evgeny Levchenko
Anatoli Tymoschuk
Denny Landzaat
Kiki Musampa
Ronald de Boer
Roy Makaay
Thomas Buffel
Nacho Novo
Shota Arveladze
Robert van der Weert
Nordin Wooter
Lorenzo Amoruso
Fernando Ricksen

The latter just had a few exciting weeks. He became the first Dutchman ever to be featured in Rangers' Hall of Fame, Arena Sport in Edinburgh released the English edition of his book and, in between, he finally married Veronika. And yet, he doesn't look tired at all! That is, he tells me, because he decided to take his foot off the gas pedal. Easy does it, from now on.

"He has finally accepted it," says Veronika. "After six months. I'm happy with it, so we can move on."

"I had to," adds Fernando. "How long can one wait for that phone call from the hospital, in which they confess that they were wrong? That phone call will never happen. It is what it is. I have MND and I have to deal with it. Acceptance is a start. And remember that I am not just dealing with myself. I have to think about my family too. We're in this together. And I should not just think about Fernando. I have to think about Veronique and Bella too."

But he doesn't want to look too much ahead. He doesn't want to picture himself in a wheelchair. He doesn't want to think about the day Veronika has to wash him. He knows it will come, but he hopes it will happen step by step. And very slowly.

He is still capable of driving a car. "I am very grateful for that. Although I know that it won't stay like this forever. But for now, I am still enjoying it. For as long as it lasts."

Today, at the press conference for his testimonial, he is in relatively good shape. But I have to add that he had sixteen (!) hours of sleep. Anyway, he is in good spirit. Not to say: fighting spirit.

He speaks monotonously and slower than before, that is unmistakably true, but he still manages to crack the occasional joke. And he is so much looking forward to be on a pitch again, in his football boots. "I hope my body allows me to kick a ball or two. That would be fantastic."

Less fantastic is the fact that Frank de Boer, Arthur Numan, Michael Mols, Bert Konterman, Patrick Kluivert, Clarence Seedorf and a few Russians won't be able to make it. And Dick Advocaat, who is abroad, can't be there either. But hey, there's enough All Stars left for one hell of a match!

Willem van Hanegem will make his appearance too. The former Feyenoord star, who Brian Glanville thought was the best player at the 1974 World Cup in West-Germany, has always admired Fernando, before, during and after their stint at the Dutch national team, where De Kromme ('The Crooked One') was assistant trainer. The two had previously worked together in Alkmaar, where coach Van Hanegem was in charge. Despite having been one of Holland's toughest players ever, Van Hanegem is a very sensitive man. When confronted with even the tiniest bit of misery, he starts crying. Fernando's illness came as a shock to him and he really sees it as his task to be there for him. Hence his appearance as coach of the All Stars.

Martin Masset, managing director of Fortuna Sittard Football Club, then says that he appreciates the fact that, after all his foreign adventures, Fernando decided to return to the green & yellows. "It's obvious he did that to help the club. So now it's our turn to help him!" And, as he sticks a fork into a piece of *vlaai* (a local type of cake, topped with cherries): "Normally we sell nine tickets online. Now the counter is on 500 already – and we've only just started!"

Among the fans who bought a ticket are quite a few Scots. That doesn't surprise him at all. Masset: "A while back I was in Glasgow with Fernando. Couldn't believe my eyes. It was like walking around with Robbie Williams! They absolutely love him over there." Grinning: "I still remember that road worker, who was just doing his work. 'Holy fuck,' he yelled, 'it's Ricksen!' I think that sums it up."

MAY 25, 2014: **Guard of honour**

"Ricksen?? Fernando Ricksen?? Well, good luck, pal!"

That's what a colleague at [regional newspaper] *Limburgs Dagblad* said to Roel Wiche, as he was leaving the editorial room to go to Glasgow, for a feature on the Rangers star. The year was 2003.

"So yes, my knees were trembling," he now says. "I expected a monster, but was confronted with a friendly, down-to-earth guy who was even more nervous than me!"

After supplying the Dutch reporter with snacks and drinks, he took him for a ride in his SUV. And something similar happened four years later, in the beautiful Russian city of Saint Petersburg. Wiche still recalls the stunning woman in stilettos who posed with Fernando for the photographer that accompanied the journalist. "He then told me about the injections he was getting, in his fight against alcoholism. It was quite a confession."

Another seven years later and Roel Wiche is attending the match between Fortuna Sittard and Fernando's All Stars. He writes about it, of course. This is his report:

2.30 PM: Is this going to be A Day To Remember, for Fernando Jacob Hubertina Henrika Ricksen? Will it be a heavy one? It's quite obvious that he won't forget this 25th of May, 2014. Accompanied by his little daughter Isabella, who doesn't leave him alone for a second, he greets all those fellow warriors from years gone by. There's Michael Reiziger, a bit chubbier than in his heydays and there's Roy Makaay, Giovanni van Bronckhorst and former Fortuna aces Mark van Bommel and Kevin Hofland. Only a few days ago, Shota Arveladze and Anatoli Tymoschuk were in the Champions League Final in Lisbon, but they didn't want to miss this tribute in Sittard for the world. Only Lorenzo Amoruso didn't show up. Rumour has it that he had 'something' to explain to his wife. "I know enough," grins Fernando. Of course he does. He and the Italian glamour boy spent many a night in Glasgow's vibrant night life.

3.38 PM: There they are, the first tears of the day. It's Willem van Hanegem who breaks, emotionally, as he shakes hands with his former pupil Fernando. The latter joins him – and both hard men cry. "Fernando was a tough bastard," Van Hanegem explains, as the tears have dried up. "A pain in the ass, actually. But a very good football player too!"

4.13 PM: Another very emotional moment. Fernando meets Fortuna steward Bert Paardekooper, who also suffers from MND. Although Fernando's illness hasn't progressed as much as Bert's, he's already been to the photo studio for the national MND awareness campaign. One day, Fernando's face will appear on bus stops too, with the line "By now, I am dead. Join the fight against a merciless disease."

5.38 PM: Kick-off is at seven, but Ricksen wants to inspect the pitch already. He also wants to see the Fortuna youth, kids at the age of 15, 16. They are the guys he used to train, before he was diagnosed with MND. Boyd, Job, Amar, Clint, Martijn, Stijn, Francis, Luc, Faissal, Sean, Giel, Dean... Do they already know how cruel life can be?

6.51 PM: The 3000 fans who bought a ticket for this special match, enter the stands. There's Union Jacks on the N-side. From Ayr, a coachload of Rangers fans has made the 22 hour journey to Sittard. In a specially made testimonial paper, an advert by Rangers reads: 'Keep your fighting spirit and stay strong.' As the man himself enters the pitch, through a guard of honour, Fortuna's hard core fans unfold an enormous banner. It has Fernando on it, wearing the colours of all the professional clubs he played for, plus the orange jersey of the Dutch national team.

7.07 PM: It looks like it's going to be a testimonial like all others when the opponent isn't called Bayern Munich (the writer is referring to Johan Cruyff's testimonial in 1978, when the Krauts slaughtered them: 0-8 – ed.). Slow motion football (Wooter), hilarious misses (Arveladze) and a world class goal (Novo, from the halfway line). But there is only one thing everybody's waiting for: the appearance of Fernando Ricksen.

8.42 PM: And there it is. Fernando Ricksen steps onto a football field, for the very last time. The crowd goes wild, especially when they let him score, from the penalty spot. The All Stars win, 5-2. Fernando is carried around on the shoulders of his fellow All Stars. The disc jockey plays You'll Never Walk Alone. *It's a day to remember.*

9.01 PM: Managing director Masset announces that the North Stand will be christened Fernando Ricksen Stand. Fernando wants to thank every single person in the stadium, but he can't. Too many emotions. A friend reads the words that Fernando has written back home. "Thanks for everything. Thanks to my wife and daughter, who still believe in me. With all this positive energy, I am convinced that I will make the impossible possible."

9.23 PM: Everybody wants to have his picture taken with Fernando, or so it seems. As we listen to ABBA's Fernando, *the song that gave the footballer his name, we realise that he didn't play his last game tonight. There is one more to come. The most challenging one of his life. It's the one against MND.*

MAY 26, 2014: **Highlight**

"What did you like most, yesterday?" I ask him.

"Everything."

"Everything?"

"Yes, everything. The match, the atmosphere, the fact that I saw the boys again, the christening of the Fernando Ricksen Stand..."

"And you even scored!"

"It was a good one, wasn't it?" (he jokes, as it was a bit of an act, which you are almost obliged to do when the main character doesn't have the strength to kick a ball properly – ed.)

"A goal in your very last game."

"Yeah, how do they say it? You have to stop at your peak?"

"That's what they say."

"Then that's exactly what I did. I stopped at my peak."

AUGUST 19, 2014: **Ice Bucket Challenge**

Fernando spends the entire Summer in Turkey. Not for a holiday, but to see whether the hot climate is any good for his tortured muscles. It's an experiment. And not a bad one. He sends me one app after the other, in which he says that the weather is perfect. Three weeks ago he celebrated his 38th birthday, under a totally blue sky.

"You have to come over," he writes. And: "Bring your pencil with you. There's a lot of copies of *Fighting Spirit* to sign here. You won't believe how many people are reading it on the beach!"

Although the experiment isn't finished yet, Fernando and Veronika have been searching for a school for Isabella already. They even found one. "A Russian one. That's better for her than anything else."

As I said: that is not what he said. It's what he wrote. Because his voice is even more, well, let's say viscous than before. It's getting more and more difficult to understand him, especially when you're not sitting face to face. Very frustrating. Especially for him.

So WhatsApp is the solution. For now. Because his fingers are more and more crooked...

Veronika, in the meantime, is exhausted. Because recently, Fernando was nowhere to be found. For three weeks in a row.

Yes: three weeks!

She panicked. And called me. "I'm so scared!" she screamed. "So scared that something has happened to Nando! You know him, Vincent! You know that he is prone to all kinds of trouble! He just left, Vincent! Just like that! Walked through the door and that was it! He's gone and I don't know where he is! And we didn't even have a fight or so!"

I asked her if she had called the police. She hadn't. "But this shouldn't last any longer, because then I'm gonna call them! This isn't normal, Vincent!"

Spot on.

"And he didn't even take a bag with him! Nothing! Just his car keys! What if he drove the car into a tree? I am so worried! Has he called you, by chance?"

No, he didn't call me once, in those three weeks. And all of a sudden he was back with his family, in Turkey. Just like that. With a few scratches in his face. He had been to Holland, because he 'needed some rest'.

"Do you know what he has done here?" I asked her.

"No, but I have an idea," she answered. And that was probably the same idea that I had.

"But please don't bring the topic up, Vincent!"

"I won't say a word, Veronika."

"Better talk to him about the Ice Bucket Challenge."

"The WHAT?" apps Fernando, as I tell him about this phenomenon.

"It's an internet thing. If somebody challenges you, you have to throw a bucket full of ice water over your head and have it filmed. If you can't do that within the next 24 hours, you'll have to donate money to an MND organisation."

"Cool."

Pun intended?

I app him some background information. The Ice Bucket Challenge is an fund-raising initiative by former baseball player Peter Frates, who himself is an MND victim.

"Any idea how many celebrities have done this challenge already? Loads! Lewis Hamilton, Oprah Winfrey, Lady Gaga, Leonardo DiCaprio, Justin Timberlake..."

"Any football players too?"

"Too many to mention! Robin van Persie, Neymar, Cristiano Ronaldo, the entire PSV squad... And Vincent de Vries himself. So hereby, I challenge you. It's a bucket full of ice water or you'll have to pay!"

"Within 24 hours, you said?"

"Within 24 hours."

The clip arrives faster than that. Much faster. I see Fernando, dancing on flipflops on the balcony of his Turkish apartment. Thumbs up. And who cares that the Turkish guy who holds the bucket, doesn't pour ice water over Fernando, but cubes? Nobody. Within a few hours, more than half a million people have seen (and appreciated) the little piece of film already. Thumbs up – again.

SEPTEMBER 2, 2014: **Sepp Blatter (1)**

"Hey Fernando, guess who sent us an invitation!"

"No idea. Who is it?"

"Guess!"

"How the fuck do I know?"

"Just mention one name!"

"Can't think of a name."

"Sepp Blatter! He wants to meet you at the FIFA HQ in Zürich!"

"Cool. When are we going?"

"Somewhere in November."

"Super cool. Tell him my suitcase is packed already."

"Don't forget to show up nicely dressed! In a smart suit or so."

"Nah, I was more thinking about a John de Wolf shirt (way back in the Nineties, former Feyenoord and Wolves player De Wolf promoted shirts that looked like they were made by a drunken chimpanzee on acid – ed.), with white socks and adidas shower slippers."

SEPTEMBER 12, 2014: **Guinea pig**

The Turkish sun has done him good. That's the first thing that springs to mind, when I meet him again after three long months. He even walks better than before, I notice.

"Turkey was great," he admits, as we walk towards the Van Eyk Hotel in Maaseik, where we have an appointment with

Joep Schreuder, for [Dutch tv programme] *Studio Sport.* "And no muscle problems at all. Weird, eh? I even swam in the sea, every day! And of course I played with Bella. A lot."

"And what went through your head, when you did that?"

"An awful lot. But I've decided to stay positive and optimistic. Bella deserves that. And maybe we still have many years in front of us. Many years together."

"Wow. You're REALLY in good spirit!"

"It even feels as if I have more strength in my fingers. Look at them! They're not as crooked as they were, right?"

Yet, he is not going back to Turkey. After all, it was more difficult to live there than expected. That school for Bella, for instance, wasn't as good as they thought.

As he tells me this, I realise that I am quite capable of understanding him. Okay, the voice still isn't what it should be, but sitting in front of him, looking at his mouth, helps a lot.

"It's all thanks to the Russian medicines," he says.

"Russian medicines?"

"Yeah, some kind of suppository. Veronique's family gave it to me. They arranged it, via some kind of Russian doctor. It was a bit risky though."

"Why risky?"

"Doctors in the Netherlands don't like it. They discourage the use of it."

"Because of possible side effects?"

"Yes. But hey: what's the point? I'll die anyway!"

"You can't wait until they have something safer?"

"I don't think I have enough time for that. And I refuse to die without having tried as much as possible."

"So in a way you're some kind of a guinea pig."

"It's the last straw, Vincent. Or at least one of the last."

"Anyway, good to see you're doing better now."

"Yeah, but let's not be too premature. In four months time, we hope to know more."

This doesn't sound too bad. After all, he thought he was going to die within four months after the diagnosis. And that would have been a while back now.

"Is this a breakthrough when it comes to battling MND?"

"Oh no. I will never be able to become my old self again. I will never be able to do everything I could do before the diagnosis again."

"Never?"

"Never. My voice, to start with, will be fucked forever. I simply hope I can stabilize things a bit. That would make me a happy man already."

"And Turkey is no longer an issue?"

"No," he says, scooping some froth off his cappuccino and putting it next to his cup, "for the time being we stay in Maaseik. But who knows, maybe one day we'll leave for Spain. Plenty of sun there too."

"You do have a house there, right?"

"Yes, in Náquera, close to Valencia. But it is in Graciela's name, so..."

Graciela, of course, is his ex-wife.

He then asks me for a favour. "Before we have that *Studio Sport* interview..."

"Yes. What about it?"

"Can you tell the bloke that I want to talk about everything but Bella. I have no problems chatting about sickness, death and addiction, but please not about my little baby. I don't want to cry on telly. Not again!"

"No worries, I'll fix it. Anything else?"

"Have you seen my new tattoos? I had a few more done in Turkey."

"Was there any spot left at all?"

"Well, I had to search for it, to be honest. But I found some empty skin. Look!"

He shows me his calves. On the left one I see the club crest of Zenit Saint Petersburg with the addition 'UEFA Cup Winner 2008', on the right there is the Rangers emblem, with five stars.

"Nice, eh?" he grins. And: "My back will be next."

"Can we film them?" the *Studio Sport* reporter asks, a little bit later.

"Of course," is the answer. "Wanna film the one on my tummy too?"

"What's on your tummy then?"

"A beautiful text." And as he lifts his shirt, we read: 'I am a warrior, a warrior with fighting spirit. I will never give up and never surrender.'

"I wanted something that I stand for," he explains.

"And this," the reporter asks, although he does know the answer already, "is typically Fernando Ricksen?"

"Yes. This is who I am and who I've always been."

"Always going on."

"Yes."

"Never surrender."

"Never."

"Is it true that you were in denial, right after the diagnosis?"

"Yes, but that was mainly because I didn't know how to handle the situation. I tried to run away from it. Which, of course, is impossible."

"Did it make you angry?"

"At first it did, yes."

"For what I've understood, 1500 Dutch people suffer from MND. Their average age is 55. You have just turned 38."

"Yeah, but I feel like I'm 55."

"Then, in that case... Was it just a matter of bad luck?"

"No. Maybe it was meant to be."

He looks at Veronika and Isabella, who are walking down the street, a few floors below us. He then waves at them and they wave back.

I look at his mouth. The lips are at twenty to four again.

OCTOBER 21, 2014: **Sepp Blatter (2)**

It rains in Zürich. In fact, in rains so heavily that the cab driver almost misses the exit to our hotel on Orellistraße.

Fernando couldn't care less. He is happy anyway. Happy to meet the most important man in football tomorrow, at the FIFA HQ on Dreiwiesenstraße. Not one single second he had thought of turning down the invitation, although lots of people asked him to do so. “Of course not,” he says, as we check in at the super posh Sorell Hotel Zürichberg. “How big are the chances of a simple guy like me meeting a man like that? This is something extraordinary! Controversial? Controversial my ass! He is the president of my world, the world of football. Therefore I respect him.”

“But do you understand the fact that others may have difficulties with you shaking hands with him?”

“No. Besides: what do they want me to do?”

“You could throw him into a pool, like you did with that Rangers chairman.”

“No way.”

As we enter the hotel restaurant, a few hours later, Fernando is still talking about it. About the respect he has for Sepp Blatter.

“I’ll never forget the fact that he was the first hot shot in football to buck me up.”

Some fifteen minutes later, Veronika is cutting his meat. Because despite some good recent test results – his lung capacity went from 50 percent to a staggering 99 percent! – he still can’t do everything. Like cutting meat.

“That’s why I am still around,” she smiles. “Although Nando doesn’t want me to do every single thing for him.”

“No,” he adds. “I don’t want to get lazy.”

And then he shuts up, as Veronika puts a piece of venison into his mouth.

OCTOBER 22, 2014: **Sepp Blatter (3)**

"What do you think?" I ask Fernando "Is he going to give us a super expensive watch, like the twenty FIFA representatives got at the World Cup in Brazil? Or just a cheap keyring?"

"I can do with a new watch," he answers with a smile.

I can see that he is nervous.

"Of course I am nervous! This is like meeting Barack Obama – or Vladimir Putin!

We are here without a camera crew. Exactly as Blatter's assistant Bernd Fisa – yes, Fisa from the FIFA – had requested. "Mister Blatter wants to have a real chat with Fernando, not an interview. That's why it is listed in his diary as a private visit. This shouldn't be a media event."

To kill the time as we are waiting to be invited into the presidential room, Fernando and Isabella are playing tag. It doesn't really help, to be honest. Fernando gets more and more nervous. And it doesn't help that minutes later he is facing the most powerful man in football.

The two shake hands, but Fernando obviously isn't at ease. "It's a small man, but at the same time he's huge!" he'll say, later that day.

Blatter asks him how he feels. Fernando says that thanks to the Russian medicines and loads of vitamins, minerals and antioxidants, he is relatively fine. "If things stay the way they are now, I'm happy."

Blatter shines. "You're still that football player, aren't you? The one that never wants to lose."

"Exactly," he answers, as Isabella jumps on his lap for the umpteenth time. "And thank God I don't really know how losing feels. It hardly happened. And in the Dutch national team not even once!"

Blatter looks at his printed Wikipedia page and says: "I am envious of your career. Champions with Glasgow Rangers, champions in Russia, European successes... What a difference with me! I was a fast forward..."

No pun intended!

"...but that's basically all I was: fast. I've never won a big prize."

"Yeah, I hate to lose," says Fernando.

Blatter pokes FIFA's chief medical officer Jiri Dvorak, who is sitting next to him, in the ribs and says: "He really has a fighting spirit, our Fernando."

And there he said it!

We brought him some presents, but weren't really sure when to give them. But now that he's said the magic words, we don't hesitate any longer. So, together with some Belgian chocolates, we present him with two books: *Fighting Spirit* and *Vechtlust*, AKA the original *Fighting Spirit* in Dutch. He opens the Dutch one, flicks through it and starts reading out loud.

"De eerste bierglazen..."

It sounds as if he owns a pub on Amsterdam's famous Leidseplein, or Eindhoven's Stratumseind. This man really has a talent for languages!

"Yeah, that's a nice chapter," laughs Fernando. "And so is the rest of the book."

"But his drinking days are over," I say to Blatter.

"Yep," Fernando admits. "Only water for me."

And then Sepp Blatter grabs Fernando Ricksen's hand. It's the moment he, the old man, has been waiting for. He is about to tell why he invited the tragic footballer.

"We are one big family, Fernando. And that's why we are going to help you."

Fernando looks a bit confused.

And then Blatter tells him about a new initiative by the FIFA, the UEFA and the KNVB (the Dutch football organisation – ed.): the Fernando Ricksen Foundation. "To support you in your battle against this disease."

"Thanks..." is all Fernando can say.

And then the 78 year old FIFA president rises from his chair. He walks a few steps towards Isabella, who is playing with a ball, and... joins her!

"Look at him!" whispers Fernando. "He is a winner too!" And indeed, the old men use all kinds of feints, basically every trick in the book, to get the ball past the toddler. It would have made fantastic television.

Ten minutes later, after Blatter has left the room, Fernando gets his much anticipated FIFA presents: an adidas ball and a pennant, with his name and today's date, in golden letters.

"This is even better than an expensive watch," he says.

And he means it.

NOVEMBER 10, 2014: **Johan Cruijff**

"Look," says Fernando, as we are walking through the outskirts of Como, Italy, on a particularly rainy day. "Do you see that yellow sign? It's the 14 rules of Johan Cruijff. You can see them at every Cruyff Court."

Fourteen, as the Dutch legend used to play with number 14. Oh, and the man was born as Johan Cruijff, but for commercial purposes / international use he changed that into Cruyff. Just like Feyenoord, which was originally called Feijenoord.

As we get closer, I read the rules. All fourteen of them.

1 TEAMPLAYER. To accomplish things, you have to do it together.

2 RESPONSIBILITY. Take good care of things as if it was your own.

3 RESPECT. Respect one another.

4 INTEGRATION. Involve others in your activities.

5 INITIATIVE. Dare to try something new.

6 COACHING. Always help each other within a team.

7 PERSONALITY. Be yourself.

8 SOCIAL INVOLVEMENT. Crucial in sports, and even more so in life in general.

9 TECHNIQUE. The basics.

10 TACTICS. Know what to do.

11 DEVELOPMENT. Sports develop body and soul.

12 LEARN. Try to learn something new every day.

13 PLAY TOGETHER. An essential part of the game.

14. CREATIVITY. The beauty of sports.

"Imagine the sign on a Ricksen Court," I hear next to me, as the rain is doing a drum solo on my umbrella. "For sure it would be a lot smaller. I have only one rule: *Do anything you want.*"

You'll find Cruyff Courts everywhere. It's an initiative by the Cruyff Foundation: small football pitches to be used by street kids. Including the ones whose parents don't have enough money to send their children to a real football club.

Today a Cruyff Court is opened in Northern Italy, in Como. And Fernando is invited as the eponym's special guest.

The two have met before, many many moons ago. Fernando: "It was in 1997, when I won one of the most valuable individual prizes in Dutch football. I became Rookie of the Year, as chosen by the editors and readers of [leading Dutch football weekly] *Voetbal International.* I was ahead of guys like Jon Dahl Tomasson, Boudewijn Zenden, Mario Melchiot and George Boateng, to name a few. And, to make things even better, the prize was given to me by none other than the mighty Johan Cruijff. So in order not to look like a provincial jerk, I bought some new clothes for the occasion: a white shirt with a black, sleeveless leather waistcoat. Well, it was the nineties. And yes, it did make me look like a provincial jerk. 'If you continue like this,' Cruijff told me, 'you have a great future ahead of you.' I think I nodded, or maybe I said yes. Definitely no more than that. For this was the one and only Johan Cruijff, the greatest Dutch footballer of all time. And in the presence of someone like Cruijff, even Fernando Ricksen is quiet."

"Very impressive," Cruijff himself says a bit later, as we are having lunch at the majestic Villa d'Este hotel. "And very good that he is here, today, with us. It's very tempting to do absolutely nothing anymore, after getting a diagnosis like Fernando got. But that wouldn't get him anywhere. That wouldn't get anybody anywhere. He travels around so he can tell about this terrible illness, give it its own face. I admire his way of thinking, I really do."

Fernando's smile is also caused by the fact that he is standing on familiar turf. Each year, way back in the Seventies, the Ricksen Family went to Lake Como, for their holidays. "Up to five weeks in a row," he remembers. "And I absolutely loved it. That is: after I'd seen the San Siro stadium. Otherwise I would be completely pissed off. My mother knew it, so it was off to Milan, right on the very first day. In that case, she saved my vacation – and that of the rest of the family, haha."

Years and years later, he was on the San Siro pitch, playing professional football. With Glasgow Rangers. A Champions League game in 2005, against Inter. "Because of a UEFA punishment we had to play in an empty stadium, but I couldn't care. My childhood dream had come true."

Stefano Borgonovo shared – and lived – the same dream. As a team mate of the famous Dutch triumvirate – Marco van Basten, Ruud Gullit, Frank Rijkaard – he ran on the San Siro pitch, in the famous *rossonero* shirt of AC Milan. Later, he played for Fiorentina, Pescara and Udinese. And in June 2013, he died. Motor Neurone Disease. The same illness that is currently trying to strangle Fernando.

"I have always admired him – and will continue to do so," says Chantal Borgonovo, Stefano's widow. "He was a fantastic human being, a family man without the excesses that are so popular among modern-day football players. He was different. Not big-headed at all. That's why I loved him."

And that's (also) why this Cruyff Court in Como is named after Stefano Borgonovo. And that, in itself, is why fellow MND-patient Fernando Ricksen is here, rubbing shoulders with his childhood hero Johan Cruijff. Admiration galore, on this wet day in the north of Italy.

"He truly was a special man," says Bernd Fisa, one of Stefano's best friends. "The first time I saw him, he was already completely paralysed. Couldn't get out of bed, couldn't move at all. Couldn't speak either. He had a special computer which he could only control with his eyes. I was amazed when I saw it. What a fighter this man was!"

Chantal sees a lot of similarities between her Stefano and our Fernando. "When I saw him on tv, talking about his disease, it was like watching Stefano. The two are so alike!"

"That's one of the reasons why we're glad that he is here today," adds Bernd. "And with Johan Cruijff as an added bonus. It's like having Christmas, Easter and the World Cup Final on one and the same day!"

"Of course I'm here," says Fernando. "Yes, it's true, for once I am out of my comfort zone. Normally I don't do much on a day, just one thing. It has to fit in my tight schedule of eating, taking medicines, and having a nap. But I simply felt I had to be here."

'Here', in Como. Reunited with the great Johan Cruijff,

seventeen years since that legendary Rookie of the Year moment. And it feels good, seeing the former number 14 of Ajax, Barcelona and, er, Feyenoord again. The two chat - and chat and chat. Not just Johan, no, Fernando too! Despite his weak voice he keeps on telling his idol things. About his career, about his illness and about little Isabella, the love of his life. He even manages NOT to cry, as images of a very sick Stefano are shown on a big screen. "Thank God I didn't," he says afterwards. "I have a stupid face when I cry. That's because the muscles are tightening up. Once again: I really look like shit when I cry, so I'm glad I didn't."

He is also glad about something else. "Johan didn't remember our first meeting. Which was fine by me, as I looked like a complete jerk, back then. That leather singlet: so stupid!!"

On a more serious note: "But what a man, our Johan. Always thinking in solutions, never in problems. And always positive. Just like me. I refuse to be down, to give up, to surrender. I'll keep going, for as long as I can. It's something I have to do, for my family. I have to be there for them, show them my famous fighting spirit. It's also something I have to do back for them. Veronique saved me from the pool of vodka I was drowning in. I have to be there for her now, she simply deserves that. Besides: negative people die faster. I am the living proof of that!"

Johan Cruijff and handicapped people, it's a well-known combination. Ever since that first unlucky little boy from the neighbours, in Los Angeles. He never came out of the house, was more or less turning into a pot plant. Until Cruijff stepped in. He took the kid out and started to play football with him.

The little fella completely thrived. Mission accomplished.

This one/off eventually led to the birth of the Cruyff Foundation, an organisation that wants to give children self-confidence and pleasure through sports. Hence the more than two hundred Cruyff Courts, all over the globe.

"It's a fantastic initiative from a fantastic man," says Fernando, in between chats with AC Milan legend Franco Baresi and Inter ace Javier Zanetti. "Yep, I know I'm only here because I share an illness with Stefano. Otherwise I wouldn't have been invited. But I don't care. That's the way it is. So please, don't feel sorry for me."

NOVEMBER 11, 2014: **Stress (1)**

"The fucking bitch..."

"What's the matter, Fernando?"

"She seized my football pension!"

"Who? Graciela?"

"Yes! Why? That's not normal, is it? It's my only income! I am about to die and she tries to steal the last bit of cash that I have!"

"Any idea why?"

"To create stress. So that I die even faster."

NOVEMBER 26, 2014: **Stress (2)**

They're all here.

Loes Leinarts, widow of Fortuna's factotum John, who spent 55 years of his life at the club.

Arthur Hoyer, former player and current snackbar owner who still owns the title European Club Top Scorer of Fortuna Sittard, thanks to his two goals against Wisła Kraków.

Frans Thijssen of Ipswich Town and Nottingham Forest fame, who also played for Fortuna.

Andy Loi, the Fortuna fan who made an enormous Fernando Ricksen banner.

Jan Notermans, who used to play for Fortuna '54, the predecessor of Fortuna Sittard, and won 25 caps with the Dutch national team.

Bert van Marwijk, father-in-law of Mark van Bommel, but also the 'Oranje' coach during the 2010 World Cup final in South Africa (which the Dutch lost to Spain, 1-0).

Mark van Bommel himself.

And Kevin Hofland.

They're all here to witness the presentation of *Nao Veure* ('Go Ahead', in dialect), a book that celebrates 60 years of football under the moniker of Fortuna. They're all here – minus one.

Fernando Ricksen.

I noticed it immediately, as he opened the door of his home in Maaseik. I was going to pick him up, but it was obvious that he wouldn't be able to make it. The look in his eyes... Hardly any life in it.

"I'm empty," he confessed a few minutes later, sitting on the couch with his head between his knees. "I wish I wasn't sick. The situation drives me insane."

He was frustrated, he said. Frustrated about the fact that by now, his fingers were so crooked that he couldn't even lift a tea cup anymore. Or a glass of water.

But more to the point, he was frustrated about the fact that Veronika had left him. With Isabella. Packed their suitcases and left for Russia, after yet another row.

"This is stressing me out completely, Vincent. Although I'm sure she'll come back."

"And what if she doesn't?"

"No idea. Maybe I go to my mother."

"Can you still cope with it?"

"Of course."

"Is there anything I can do for you?"

"No, thanks. I'm just going to sleep. I'm tired, so tired..."

"I'll let you. Take care, buddy."

"Please say hi from me, to all the people at Fortuna. And tell them I'm sorry."

"I will."

"And greetings to everyone."

"Oh, speaking about greetings... Ronald Hamming sends his best wishes. He also wants to point out that his goal against Telstar, in 1994, wasn't as easy as you said it was, in the book."

"C'mon, everybody could have made that one! Even me, in my current state."

DECEMBER 9, 2014: **Sauna**

The days spent at his mother's have done him good. He is a relatively happy man again, as the following WhatsApp conversation proves.

"Did I tell you about the German sauna I visited with some Fortuna players, once in a while?"

"Yes you did."

"And that at some stage we had a gold bathrobe made for one of the guys?"

"Yeah. Great fun."

"Last night, all of a sudden I had to think about something else that happened."

"What?"

"Remember the time I was in Maastricht, with a couple of guys from Fortuna?"

"The time you drank a bit too much?"

"Yep, that one. After the pubs closed, we went to one of those German saunas."

(German saunas, by the way, are not just there for people to enjoy a steam bath. They are full of naked women who want to dance the horizontal lambada with you. Sometimes you have to pay them, other times the service is included. Like the 'all you can eat' joints, these are 'all you can...' Well, you get the picture – ed.)

"And what happened?"

"Flashing lights behind me. Polizei!"

(That's German for 'Police!' – ed.)

"The guys in the car went nuts, as you can understand."

"I can fully understand that."

"Also because I didn't stop. In fact, I took off, full throttle."

"Jesus..."

"The guys were really panicking. They saw themselves ending up in a German jail."

"And?"

"I was forced into the kerb. And handcuffed."

"Ouch."

"But there's more to come. At the police office, they forced me to have a blood test. To see if I had been on the booze."

"Ah."

"But I was so plastered, that I couldn't even walk anymore!"

"Man, man, man..."

"And the guys were completely stressed out."

"So you ended up in jail?"

"No! I got away with just a fine. Which I had to pay on the spot. If I couldn't pay it there and then, they would put me behind bars."

"What a story."

"So I told one of the guys: hand me my little Gucci bag!"

"Because?"

"That's where I had my cash. They never believed I could pay the 1000 euro fine. But I did. The little Gucci bag was stuffed with 50 euro notes. So I took out 1500 euro and threw it on the table. 'You can leave the tip!' I yelled."

"That's quite brilliant."

"Yeah. The guys were in stitches."

Talking about laughing: that's what Fernando himself can do too. Veronika and Isabella are still in Saint Petersburg, at her mother's house, but at least he and his wife are on speaking terms again. He even thinks about paying them a visit.

"But don't tell anybody! It has to be a surprise."

2015:
The Awareness

JANUARY 13, 2015: **Golden Ball**

Fernando is back from Russia, but things between him and Veronika are not yet as they should be. That's why she didn't accompany him to the Golden Ball Ceremony in Zürich, Switzerland. Instead, he went with his pal Roy Knez, with whom he has been living for the past few weeks. Better with a male friend than completely on his own.

I ask him what the thought about the event.

"Fantastic, absolutely fantastic! The emotion on Ronaldo's face when they called out his name, so fantastic!"

"That was the highlight of the evening?"

"Without a doubt. But it was also great that I managed to talk to Arjen Robben, Clarence Seedorf and Ruud Gullit. Plus Thierry Henry, Christian Karambeu, Alessandro del Piero and Michel Platini. They all came up to me for a chat."

"And what did they say?"

"Robben thought I was very brave to be there. And Clarence said that I can always call him. He has seen what happened to Borgonovo, so he knows a thing or two about MND."

"And how about your friend Blatter?"

"He hugged me."

"And did he say something as well?"

"Yes. He said: 'I give you all my energy to help you.' I can assure you: that gave me a lump in my throat. Oh, and Carlo Ancelotti, who as you know played with Borgonovo, asked me to meet him in Madrid."

"And what did you say?"

"Somewhere in April."

JANUARY 18, 2015: **Power Plate**

The amount of people who say they can cure MND patients by using their magic potion... There are so many of them. And they all know how to get to Fernando, it seems. Super medicines, therapies, ointments, whatever... We don't even answer them anymore. It's too many of them. Besides, Fernando doesn't trust the majority of them. Take that holistic program based on jumping on a bellicon trampoline... Not for Fernando, as you would have guessed.

Still, he doesn't just sit and wait, doing nothing. Because he knows his days are numbered, he checks the internet on an almost daily basis. And all of a sudden...

"Hey, Vincent, listen to this! A Power Plate."

He apps me a photo of some kind of a vibrating platform.

"Sounds ideal to me," he says. Without using your muscles, you give your blood circulation a kick up the arse. It also helps to improve your coordination and stability. It's just the price that bothers me. The bloody thing costs 20,000 euro. Could you maybe get in touch with the manufacturer? Maybe they are able and willing to give me one. In return I can give them some great publicity. Because I'm convinced it works."

Back in Glasgow again. At Ibrox, to be precise. Exactly a year later. Only this time there are no tears. On the contrary: Fernando is very cheerful. This, because he is very excited to announce the line-up for his forthcoming testimonial. A match in Glasgow, this time.

We are welcomed by Andy Goram and Barry Ferguson, who still support Fernando wherever they can. And Fernando himself is, as said, proud to announce that the likes of Stefan Klos, Arthur Numan, Jörg Albertz, Peter Løvenkrands, Ronald de Boer, Marvin Andrews, Marco Negri, Gennaro Gattuso, Gordon Durie, Thomas Buffel, Bert Konterman, Michael Mols, Nacho Novo and Alex Rae will cross proverbial swords with people like Dave Beasant, Teddy Sheringham, Darren Anderton, Kevin Hofland, Kiki Musampa, Denny Landzaat, Paul Bosvelt, Kenneth Perez, Ronald Waterreus, James Beattie and Charlie Miller.

Fernando talks his head off. But he is also quiet, when he hears that, off all clubs, Celtic has donated 10,000 pounds. Celtic, the green and white arch rivals who, after all, lost their own John Cushley and Jimmy Johnstone to MND.

"Unbelievable," he then says, "that so many fans bought a ticket for this game. If we sell out, you're talking about an audience of 40,000. That's a bigger crowd than at a One Direction concert! And, mind you, there are five of them – and I am on my own!"

Despite wisecracks like this, Fernando finds it difficult to talk this morning. Not because he doesn't want to – as we said earlier, he is very talkative – it's just very difficult for him to weave sentences. It's that bloody voice once again – it gets worse and worse. In a way, every sentence is a battle on its own. And the photo shoot on the pitch didn't do him much good either. He shivers, he is tired and he wants to go, earlier than expected.

He needs to have a bite to eat too. So he stuffs himself with a few *stroopwafels*, which he brought with him from the Netherlands. Stroopwafels (literally: syrup waffles) are Dutch treats, wafer cookies to be precise. It's two thin layers of chequered baked dough with syrup in between. They are delicious – open a packet of ten and it's quite likely that you have finished them before your cup of coffee is cold. As they contain a lot of sugar, they give you an energy boost as well. Which, of course, is perfect for Fernando.

JANUARY 23, 2015: **Heart of gold**

Fans come in all sizes. And we're not talking beer bellies here! We just want to point out that some fans are going the extra mile – well, make that ten miles, for some! – to support their idols. Take Linda Clark, who does security at Rangers. Donated HER ENTIRE MONTHLY SALARY to Fernando and his battle against MND. And Zoë Smith paid SIX THOUSAND POUNDS for the shirt Fernando wore at his testimonial in Sittard.

Diehard fan Pauline Glen would love to do something similar. There's only one problem: she can't spend that much money. So she had to come up with something else. And that something else turned out to be: organising special evenings to raise cash on behalf of Fernando and MND.

Tonight is such an evening. Location: The Ibrox Suite, from which we have a beautiful view over the pitch. It's truly impressive what Pauline has organised here. And she did it all by herself. That includes booking the various hosts and arranging all the items for tonight's special auction, an enormous bottle of whisky being one of them.

"I am very nervous," she confesses to Geert-Jan Jakobs, reporter of [Dutch football magazine] *Voetbal International.* The nerves aren't just caused by the event itself; she also sweats because Fernando is nowhere to been seen, while he should have been here an hour ago already. "Ah, well, Fernando is always late," she then says.

Pauline, who sports a Fernando tattoo on her arm, complete with number 2 and his signature, knows her idol since 2000, the year he swapped AZ Alkmaar for Glasgow Rangers. "I fancied him immediately," she says. "That's why I bought him a present back then: a teddy bear dressed as a Scotsman. Since that day, we are friends. Would you believe that in the beginning he was shy? Probably not. But it's true. And there is something else you have to believe from me: he has a heart of gold. Yes, he has been a nutter, but I know his soft side. Life with my son Declan hasn't always been easy, to put it mildly. But Fernando has always been there for us."

She tells that he gave her the shirt he wore at his first ever match for the Dutch national team. "He could have kept it for himself, or could have given it to an important person. But no, he chose to give it to me. Enough said."

"At a certain moment, Declan needed a warm coat," she says, as a tear drops out of her eye. "But I didn't have the money for one. So Fernando bought him one. I had to make sure though that it didn't contain feathers, as Declan suffers from asthma. You know what happened next? Fernando took the coat and went back to the shop, to find out what the coat was made of. It's just something small, but at the same time it's something big. Fernando really is one hell of a guy. A special one."

As she tells the story, more and more people enter The Ibrox Suite. "Would you believe it?" Pauline then says, all of a sudden. "We're sold out! Completely!" That's 200 Fernando fans in total, tonight at Ibrox. And they all cheer and sing and weep when the man himself shows up at last.

Former team mate and current good friend Nacho Novo is the first one to grab the microphone. And as he starts talking, there is more laughter than at a Frankie Boyle or Kevin Bridges gig. Okay, maybe not as much as when Danny Bhoy does his comedy routine but hey, let's not talk about Bhoys here, nudge nudge, wink wink. Novo is funny, as he says: "It sometimes felt as if Fernando had downed 24 espressos before going to the club for the morning training. The level of energy this guy had was out of this world!" And Michael Mols: "All I can say is: thanks Fernando! Thanks for the fact that, due to your pranks with fireworks and stuff, the value of my house dropped like a pair of trousers without elastics!"

Thumbs up from the man himself. And Mols, to us: "Look

at my arm. Goosebumps! And that's only for now. God knows what will happen tomorrow..."

JANUARY 25, 2015: **Schwalbe**

And then it's dead quiet.

A full stadium holds its breath.

What everybody feared, has finally happened.

Fernando did the kick-off. Lost his balance. Fell backwards. And lies there, flat on his back.

He died.

At least, that's what all of us think.

He died in the middle of a full football stadium, with all eyes set on him.

What a way to go!

I curse. Yes, it's one way of saying adieu, but fuck, Fernando, I can't miss you yet! None of us can. Especially Veronika and Isabella.

And then, as I squint my eyes, I see Ronald de Boer laughing. And Negri, Løvenkrands, Numan and Gattuso are in stitches too.

Is it relief?

Fact is, Fernando gets back on his feet. And the stadium explodes. As he wobbles back to the dug-out, he gets the biggest round of applause ever.

The match that follows, is a formality. Gattuso tackles. De Boer passes. Perez (twice), Novo and Sheringham, among others, score. Fernando's All Stars win, 7-4.

Five hours later, Rick Geenen still can't believe what has happened, earlier on. The former, mediocre Fortuna Sittard player, now defending the colours of EVV (the one from Echt, not the more famous one from Eindhoven, although they both play in blue and white striped shirts), keeps saying it. "I have just played with some of the greatest footballers on earth. At a sold out Ibrox. Can you believe that?" And: "Can you believe Fernando chose me for this game?"

"He could have asked so many much more famous players," adds Gino Facenna, another not-so-very-well-known face from Fortuna, who was also selected by Fernando. Facenna, who after six seasons with Fortuna Sittard swapped the club for the amateurs of SC Susteren: "Fernando isn't the scumbag some people think he is. Not at all! When he returned to Fortuna, in 2009, he helped us, young inexperienced players, with everything. He really is one hell of a guy. That's one of the reasons why I am here. It's an honour to be picked for a game like this, sure, but at the same time it feels like I'm doing something for Fernando in return. To thank him for everything he did for Rick and me."

In another corner of the Thistle Hotel's bar, Fernando looks extremely tired. "But man, it was great," he sighs – and that's not just because he was voted Man of the Match!

"What did you like most?" I want to know.

"Nothing in particular. Everything was fantastic. So good to see all those lads again."

"And now off to bed?"

"Yes, I am knackered. This will cost me a week. But it was worth it."

"But hey, what happened with that kick-off?"

"Nothing special. I tried to do a *Schwalbe* (German word for fake dive – ed.), but it wasn't very well executed. You should jump forwards, not backwards."

"Ha."

"Seriously: it was the cold, combined with the emotions. I couldn't control my muscles anymore."

"It looked very scary!"

"Possibly. But hey, that's life with MND."

"But couldn't you use your hands, as you fell?"

"Useless. I would have broken both of my arms."

"Oh dear."

"But now I have to go. Before I fall again!"

He rises from his chair, slowly, and says to nobody in particular: "Thanks for being here with me tonight. It was fantastic."

JANUARY 29, 2015: **Sepp Blatter (4)**

An e-mail from Sepp Blatter. "Pleased to hear that the testimonial in Glasgow was such as big success. It looked like not just a great sporting moment, but also a great human gesture."

JANUARY 30, 2015: **Dutch railways**

"The things that happen to me..."

"What is it this time?"

"NS (Nederlandse Spoorwegen, the Dutch railways - ed.). Not normal."

"What about them?"

"They refused to help me at Schiphol (Dutch airport which also has a train station – ed.). For assistance, I had to go to platform 2. With the elevator. But there was nobody there."

"And what happened next?"

"After a while I noticed an employee. But he said: 'I'm sorry, I don't have time.' So I asked: 'Maybe you can ask one of your colleagues if he could help me.' But..."

"Yes?"

"...he just took off! Without a word!"

"Extremely anti-social!"

"Yes. So there I was, simply hoping that somebody would see me."

"And that happened?"

"Yes. A girl who introduced herself as Margje Pieters noticed me and asked if I needed any help. She had just seen a photo of me and Blatter in *Metro* (free newspaper – ed.). What a coincidence!"

"You can say that!"

"So thanks to her I could step onto the train."

"That's nice."

"It's just that the train didn't go any further."

"The train didn't go any further?"

"No. All of a sudden there was an announcement that my train was leaving from platform 3, instead of 2. Normally that's hardly a problem. But hey, I'm not the fastest man on earth anymore. Besides, I only had one minute to change platforms!"

"Ouch."

"So off we went, the two of us. Into the elevator, to platform 3. It all went very smoothly, so I was thinking: yes, I'm gonna make it! But just as I wanted to enter the train, they closed the doors! Despite the fact that they saw me, an invalid man, approaching."

"Unbelievable."

"Unbelievable? A fucking disgrace!! Do NS really call this service??"

FEBRUARY 6, 2015: **Michele Turnu**

As Fernando's situation more or less stabilized, Michele Turnu's went downhill. In fact, the former bodybuilder got so sick, that he decides to be euthanized. Tonight.

There is just one last wish left, his soulmate Sanne van Haandel tells us. Before Michele dies, he wants to see Fernando.

So off we go, to the hospice in the Dutch town of Kerkrade. With a very nervous Fernando on the passenger seat. Nervous, because he is angry with himself that he never made an appointment, despite his promise to meet Michele after he, Fernando, didn't show up at that meet & greet in Heerlerheide, one year ago. But also nervous because he knows that today, he will look at the future Fernando.

"Although, one thing: I will never go to a hospice!"

Of course, says Sanne as we meet her, that's also one place Michele didn't want to end up. But he simply had no choice. He got weaker and weaker, especially after that trip to Colombia. "He couldn't even use his computer mouse anymore. And his throat was constantly full of phlegm. They had to suck it out, a few times per day. Each day. And on top of everything else he got pneumonia. He was coughing day and night. It was terrible."

As we enter Michele's room, we see what that bastard called MND can do to a human being. Michele, wearing an oxygen mask, is as thin as a rake. Nobody's last hours should look like this.

He can still talk though. A little bit. He tells us that he feels like a loser. He is about to give up, while he always said that he wouldn't. He would never surrender, just like Fernando. And now he's stepping out. What a pussy.

But he simply can't go on anymore. It's over.

What follows, is a chat between two MND patients without mentioning MND once. They talk about motorcycles – and the beautiful province of Limburg, where they both grew up. They tell each other jokes, they laugh a bit. It is as if they've known each other for years.

After an hour, it's finally time to say goodbye. Michele says that Fernando's visit turned out to be one of the most beautiful moments of his life.

And then he says something very, very moving.

"Fernando, I didn't make it. I will not be the person who beats MND. So please, promise me that you will be that person!"

Fernando nods, gets up and kisses Michele on the forehead. He then leaves the room, in tears.

A few hours later we hear that Michele Turnu has died, at seven past seven.

MARCH 21, 2015: **Helicopter Sunday**

Remember that one? It's the day, in 2005, that Glasgow Rangers won the title, thanks to Celtic being beaten by Motherwell, in the dying seconds of the game. It's been well documented in Fernando's autobiography *Fighting Spirit*. If you don't have a copy of that book, go and order one now! In the meantime, this is what it says about that very special, memorable day:

Not that success came easy. We really had to dig deep. We literally became champions in the last minute of the last game of the season. Celtic had been ahead five points, but in their last games they completely lost it. And because of the fact that they also lost their very last confrontation (against Motherwell, with two goals from Scott McDonald in stoppage time) while we kept winning (including the last match against Hibernian, thanks to a goal by Nacho Novo), we grabbed the trophy.

It was almost better and crazier than two years earlier, when we stayed ahead of the Hoops by one lousy goal. Yes, the 2005 title was even more extreme. That's because nobody thought we would be able to do it: nobody, including the Scottish FA. They didn't even make the effort to organise a replica of the cup with us in the stadium, just in case. So when we did the unthinkable, the buggers had to fly all the way to Motherwell's Fir Park to pick up the real trophy. By helicopter! As they landed in Edinburgh somebody noticed the green ribbons were still attached to it... What a bunch of amateurs!

"Good Lord, what a day that was!" sighs David Calderwood, owner of Cooper's Bar in Wishaw. "I still see myself invading the pitch. We were insane. I think I've been drunk for three days in a row – and I'm not exaggerating! Thinking about it: I think it was four days in a row. Yeah, well, what do you expect? It was the biggest surprise of our lives."

Fernando was Rangers' captain that day. That's why Calderwood, a Rangers season ticket holder since he was 13, wanted to have him in his pub, a watering hole that was named after another Rangers legend, Davie Cooper. Michael Mols, Marco Negri, Nacho Novo, Pieter Huistra, Charlie Miller, Bob Malcolm and Alex Rae had been there already, when Fernando finally stepped into this Rangers pub, in November 2014.

"What a day that was!" Calderwood sighs once more. "Look at this!"

He grabs his phone and shows me a photo of Fernando, pouring beer with a big grin on his face. "My hero preparing me a pint of Tennent's, isn't that amazing? And without a ridiculous amount of foam, like I got in Amsterdam. Somebody paid him 100 pound for it. Really! Unforgettable moments."

And now Fernando is back. And he doesn't leave until a few minutes after midnight. "Look at that..." Calderwood says to me, as he watches Fernando and his friend Victor Morgan heading for Main Street. "You can't call that walking anymore, can you Vincent? It's basically limping. It's going fast now – and I'm talking about the disease here. He is so much worse than four months ago. Such a fantastic athlete, back in the day. And now this. It's so cruel."

I see tears in his eyes.

"And you can hardly understand him. While four months ago, he was doing this sort of stand-up comedy routine, with a microphone. Only four months ago! You know what?"

He is really crying now.

"I hope he will be here again, in another few months time. We all do. Nights like these, that's what we live for."

And then he turns to Eddy van der Ley, who once again joined us on a trip to Glasgow.

"What the hell were you thinking? You could have been arrested!"

"I tried to be funny," Van der Ley says sheepishly. "A little joke to break the ice."

"This, young man, is a Rangers pub. And in a Rangers pub you can't say 'Fuck the Queen'!"

"Yeah, I kinda had the idea. The whole place fell silent."

"Why, do you think, there is a portrait of Queen Elizabeth on the wall?"

"I guess, er, because you like her."

"Exactly. So it's good that you apologised."

"About three or four times!"

"Yeah, that was good. And the other remark was the icing on the cake."

"Ah, you mean when I mentioned 'that shitty club in green and white'?"

"Yes. And when you started to insult the Pope. One is ALWAYS welcome to do that, in a Rangers pub!"

MARCH 31, 2015: **Goede Tijden, Slechte Tijden**

He doesn't have to think for very long.

"Raúl, who else?"

We're on our way to the match between the Netherlands and Spain, as special guests of the Dutch FA, and I have just asked Fernando who, in his eyes, is the best Spanish football player ever.

"Ever played against him?"

"Twice."

"And?"

"He didn't score. Thanks to me."

"You never lost an international match with the Dutch team, right?"

"Right. Not one."

That evening, Holland beats Spain 2-0, thanks to goals from Stefan de Vrij and Davy Klaassen. Fernando loved every minute of it. But the biggest smile on his face appears afterwards, as we walk to the car. And no, that is not because he remembers

Wesley Sneijder's invitation to come to a Galatasaray match, in the very near future. It's because we bump into Erik de Vogel and Caroline de Bruijn.

Erik de Vogel and Caroline de Bruijn?

Yes, Ludo Sanders and Janine Elschot.

Ludo Sanders and Janine Elschot?

This needs a bit of explanation, for our British readers. Erik de Vogel and Caroline de Bruijn are soap actors – and a couple in real life. They play the part of Ludo Sanders and Janine Elschot in *Goede Tijden, Slechte Tijden* ('Good Times, Bad Times'), the Dutch equivalent of *Eastenders*. Fernando watches *GTST* every single evening. So the fact that two leading characters from his favourite tv series recognise him and even want to have their picture taken with him, is beyond everything he could have wished for tonight.

Well, except for all things health-related, obviously.

APRIL 18, 2015: **Feeling ashamed**

"Can we please sit somewhere else?"

"Sure. But why?"

"Those people drive me insane."

We're in Barcelona, more precisely at Txapela, a Basque restaurant at the Passeig de Gràcia, where we eat delicious *pinchos*. And yes, I had noticed it too. As we were sitting next to the window, people stopped and looked inside. Stared. At him. Gobsmacked. It was bizarre.

I know, it's not normal to see an adult feeding another adult. And wiping his mouth. But hey, a little bit of respect please! There must be a reason for this. We don't do this for fun, you know!

"Still, it's weird," says Fernando, as we sit down at another table, far from the onlookers who treat us like monkeys from the zoo. "As a football player, I didn't care what people were thinking. But now... Even when they stare at me for just two seconds..."

"I saw it," I say. "You were shaking."

"Yes. Because I feel ashamed."

He has to accept it, he says. Because he has no other choice. But it's difficult. Very difficult.

The Power Plate, by the way, is off the wish list. He now wants a mobility scooter. Or, more to the point: he doesn't object to a mobility scooter anymore. He came to that conclusion after a long conversation with Veronika, who is back with him in Maaseik. The awful truth is: he basically can't walk anymore. So he needs the support of a mobility scooter.

But here in Barcelona, all he needs is my shoulder. Walking all of a sudden seems slightly easier than in Holland. Is it the Spanish sun? Is it the anticipation? After all, we are on our way to Camp Nou, the more than impressive stadium of Barcelona FC. Dutch website voetbaltravel.nl has invited us to attend the match against Valencia. And Fernando is full of energy. As if he wants to prove a point – is it the thought of him sitting on a mobility scooter? – he even refuses to take the elevator. He wants to climb the stairs at all costs. And yes, that goes slowly.

So we miss Luis Suárez' first minute goal. But there is still enough Messi magic left to enjoy. The Argentinian superman even scores, shortly before half time. It's magic. But not as jaw dropping as what happens next to me. Because just like anyone else, Fernando rises from his seat to applaud. Just like that, in one go.

I guess that's the power of football.

APRIL 29, 2015: **The Beauty & The Beast**

To raise more money and awareness for MND, we've come up with a plan. We are going to launch a magazine. Fernando's magazine. Hence its title: *FERNANDO.*

One of the many, many features will be an interview slash photo shoot with Fernando and Lauren Verster. Lauren is a Dutch documentary maker, who once got into trouble while doing a report on a cocaine laboratory in the jungle of Colombia. While filming, rebels of the Fuerzas Armadas Revolucionarias de Colombia (FARC) attacked the place. Bullets were flying. It was extremely exciting television.

But blonde Lauren isn't just a brave girl, she is also a beautiful one. And not just beautiful as in, er, beautiful, but *extremely* beautiful. Drop dead gorgeous. So Fernando said yes, immediately. No need for persuasion at all!

So here we are, at The Dylan, a trendy boutique hotel on Keizersgracht, one of Amsterdam's famous canals. Lauren, wearing a short beige skirt, asks, Fernando answers. What follows, is a nice conversation.

Here is that nice conversation.

The Dylan is a classy, not to say posh hotel in the pulsating heart of Amsterdam. The kind of place that's more than suitable for a (former) professional footballer and, er, moi. I mean: you didn't expect us to do the interview in a greasy spoon, did you? So off I went, on my highest heels, to the Keizersgracht, one of the city's most famous canals, for a meeting with Mister Ricksen himself. Who was already there, as I entered the lobby. Of course he was. Most men are like that, at least when they have an appointment with yours truly. I seem to have that effect on guys. But enough about me. (Thanks! – ed.) As we shook hands, I couldn't help noticing the incredible amount of tattoos on his body. The guy looks like a walking Louvre Museum!

He kindly asked me if I want one too. I kindly answered no. "Are you sure?" he continued. "Yes, I am sure," I said. Maybe I'm simply not rock & roll enough for a life-long sticker. Fernando is – or at least was. As his book Fighting Spirit *reveals, he consumed enough alcoholic beverages to drown an elephant in, threw more punches than Muhammad Ali in his prime and outnumbered Hugh Hefner when it comes to bedding lusty lasses. Hell, he once even shared a household with FOUR striptease dancers!*

That was quite a harem, big boy.

Fernando, grinning: "When I came home after training, the entire house was cleaned. I must admit: that was quite nice."

Your own personal cleaning ladies. Wearing a special uniform, I assume.

"Just a string, most of the time."

And you even shagged them.

"Not all of them."

Why not?

"I was good – but not that *good, haha. But it was great to shock people with them, once in a while."*

How did you do that?

"Entering a restaurant, with all four of them, to show off in front of my team mates and their spouses. Four gorgeous women – and not one being my own wife!"

You bastard.

"I think it was hilarious. Don't you? And I'm sure my fellow footballers were envying me. All of them!"

It was the kind of thrill you needed?

"Absolutely. I had to go out, exploring the nightlife. I sometimes even went straight from a nightclub to the training ground!"

And despite those antics, you have reached the top. Impressing!

"Yeah, but that's because I always gave it a thousand percent. Not a single coach can say that I ever cheated, when it came to doing my job. I never let my team down, never!"

But… If you hadn't been drinking and partying, you may have reached an even higher top!

"Quite possible. But then my book would have been boring."

No regrets…

"Only about snorting coke, when I played in Russia. That was a mistake. Apart from that: no regrets, Lauren."

You would do it again?

"Absolutely. Minus the Charlie, that is. And minus the headlines in the tabloids. Fuck, I hated them! I hated the rats who run – especially – the British press. They are only out to destroy you."

Which brings me to the ultimate topic: the disease that is about to destroy you. The moment you heard you have MND...

"...was the worst moment of my life. Also because the doctor wasn't very subtle in passing the message. He literally said: You have MND and you are going to die. I was totally numb, after he threw that on me."

Had you heard about MND before?

"No. So after that visit to the doctor, I started to google those three letters. And then I... I mean, that was the moment I realised..."

That's so awful. And so unexpected. You may have had dreams about ending up in the gutter or against a tree, totally pissed, or being ripped by a gold digger, but this...

"Never. And I couldn't believe it, especially because after the diagnosis I felt, well, okay. And I stayed like that for quite some time. So I assumed they had mixed up two files, at the hospital. For weeks and weeks I expected a phone call with apologies."

Must have been very surrealistic.

"Very. Mind you: at that time I was still playing professional football! Okay, not with Glasgow Rangers, but at my first club Fortuna Sittard. But it was still professional football!"

But eventually things got worse. And now you need people's help, every single day.

"That is still very difficult to accept. I wish I was independent. But I ain't – and I have to come to terms with that. It sucks, but I have no other choice. I notice that, every time I am on my own."

How?

"It's simple things, like putting on a shirt. It's basically impossible to do that myself. Those buttons... I simply can't do them up. I even need help with that. Very, very frustrating. It drives me up the wall. The body simply can't do what the mind wants. Do you have any idea how much energy it costs me to do a pair of shoelaces up? It's exhausting."

But... how can you live with that?

"I'll have to, Lauren, I don't have a choice. It all comes down to some proper preparation. For instance: I always carry a small bottle of sparkling mineral water with me. The bubbles clean my throat, so I don't choke anymore. It really works. Nevertheless, people still stare at me, as if I am some kind of attraction. Like in Barcelona, when I tried to cut and eat meat. I could hardly swallow it. Eventually, my table companion had to feed me. At the same time, I felt how everybody was looking at me. It made me so bloody nervous! I couldn't stop shaking."

And this from a man who has played in front of 100,000 people!

"It's a completely different thing, Lauren. In that restaurant, I was sooo embarrassed, you have no idea!"

You have lived life to the max, did it all, enjoyed a 24/7 party and yet, now that you are sick and not capable of doing anything anymore, you say that you are happier than ever. That sounds a bit, er, strange, to say the least.

"It's simple: I've slowed down and finally found some peace. The pressure has gone. There's a lot of it in professional football, I can assure you! And you never have time for your loved ones – your real loved ones. You're always on the move. While now, I finally have time to do nice things with my family. Take my little daughter to the zoo, that kind of things."

Like nothing has happened.

"If I don't feel too bad, I accept every invitation that I get. I watch football matches, do meet & greets with fans in pubs, have encounters with interesting people like Sepp Blatter and Johan Cruijff, who sadly died, not long ago... Moments like that make me forget that I am sick. At least for a little while. And it gives me energy – which is needed to go on."

You give me the impression of being an extremely positive person.

"I've always been like that. It's no use crying over spilt milk, as the Brits say. Sorry gets you nowhere."

Did the doctors tell you how long...

"I should have been dead within four months after the diagnosis. That was the prognosis in 2013. Well, I'm still here!"

But still... Are you scared of the inevitable?

"I'm not scared, Lauren. I've never been. Besides, being scared is just as useless as being negative."

Do you still have plans, ambitions?

"Yes: getting as old as possible. And beating that damn disease. I'm still convinced that one day, in the not so distant future, they will find a medicine against MND. I have the intention to be still around when that happens."

MAY 17, 2015: **Erik and Esther**

ADO Den Haag v PSV Eindhoven is the last game before PSV's star player, Memphis Depay, swaps the club for Manchester United. But it's quite possible that for some of my fellow spectators it will be their last game too. And that's not because they are going to United as well. No, it's because they are about to die...

We follow the match with fourteen other MND patients. Some of them have been sick for four years already, so they are living in injury time, so to say.

One of them is Erik Kamphorst, a former soldier who has been in Kosovo, Afghanistan and Bosnia. A man who knows what it means to have death leaning on your shoulder. "And that experience has helped him," his wife Esther tells us. Which doesn't mean that he has given up already, oh no. Once a warrior, always a warrior. But with the knowledge that this is one hell of an enemy. One who, in the end, always wins.

"I know I will never meet my grandchildren," says Erik. "That's the awful truth. And it hurts. It hurts like hell. Sometimes I really feel like smashing my head against the wall, I can tell you that."

"But we still appreciate the little things in life," says Esther. "Like having breakfast in the garden. Or listening to a bird whistling. The peace of mind we have, is due to the fact that we talked everything through. For instance: we planned the funeral already."

"A few weeks ago, I had dinner with the guys who are going to carry my coffin," says Erik. "How bizarre is that?"

Unlike Fernando, Erik has the spinal form of MND, which means that the disease didn't affect his speech, but his mobility. Immediately, that is. "All of a sudden I wasn't one of the fastest men running in the park anymore. That was a weird thing to notice."

"At first, we thought it was just a matter of getting older," says Esther. "I mean: he was close to 50. But then, one night, I was checking his calves and I was shocked. They used to be hard as concrete, but now they felt like porridge. And they were thinner too..."

Erik: "And then you hear you have MND. My world collapsed."

Esther: "You also said: 'That is what Fernando has! So I can't have it, because Fernando can hardly speak.' That's what you thought, back then. But you were wrong. You do have MND. So when that was clear, we immediately started to make a bucket list. Number one: watching Messi, live."

Erik: "So off we go to Barcelona, later this year. All I hope is that I still be able to walk then."

And that is something he doesn't know. Nobody does. Because MND is totally unpredictable. Like Fernando himself. Because he hardly said a word today.

JUNE 5, 2015: **Chandeliers**

The location couldn't be better.

The colossal chandeliers. The infinite stairs and corridors.

The marble lions.

The splendour.

We're in the majestic Four Seasons Hotel Lion Palace in Saint Petersburg, Russia. With its Presidential Suite where Vladimir Putin sometimes sleeps. And where Barack Obama once sat on the toilet, groaning: "Yes we can..."

No better place for a glamour shoot than this fairy tale environment. So we're very happy, excited and proud that we managed to arrange this, for our forthcoming glossy. It's gonna be a nice day, for sure, with the Ricksen family in one of the most impressive cities in the world. And on top of everything else: tomorrow is Isabella's birthday.

So we're all in a fantastic mood. Ready to do a shoot that tops the ones in magazines like *Cosmopolitan* and *Vanity Fair*. But then, all of a sudden...

"Godverdomme!"

That's me, swearing. In Dutch.

"What happened?" asks photographer Goffe Struiksma, who just arranged all his flash units.

"He's not coming!" I say.

"Who is not coming?"

"Fernando?"

"Huh? Why?"

I show him the WhatsApp. Fernando is going back to Maaseik. On his own. Despite the fact that Isabella's birthday is coming up. He just leaves her in Russia. Her and Veronika.

"I can't take it anymore," he writes. "Don't WhatsApp me anymore." And: "I won't answer anyway."

"Sometimes," says Veronika, "I think that MND is screwing up the brain too. I mean: Nando's behaviour... It's not normal, is it?"

Of course, she understands his anger and frustration. She understands that he sometimes thinks about suicide. She understands that he can get very angry, all of a sudden. Out of desperation. Maybe she would have done the same. But this... Walking out on her and his daughter, one day before her birthday...

We're having a coffee in one of the trendy bars on Nevsky Prospekt, the Champs-Élysées of Saint Petersburg. And she keeps shaking her head.

"One day before Bella's birthday," she repeats. "While he knows that for him, it can be the last one ever..."

She basically is convinced that MND destroys more than just someone's muscles. "He was never like this. Yes, we had the occasional argument. But at the same time he was always very attentive. I remember one day, six years ago, we were walking down P.C. Hooftstraat (Amsterdam's equivalent of London's Bond Street – ed.). In a shop window, I saw a 3000 euro Louis Vuitton bag that I liked. Then two months later, I got it for my birthday. While I had completely forgotten about it already! That's Nando. No, that *was* Nando. That person doesn't seem to exist anymore."

"When did the old Nando disappear?" I ask her.

"Somewhere towards the end of 2013, maybe a little bit

later. It was when he realised that he couldn't continue being a trainer for Fortuna's youth. His dream was taken away from him. That really changed him. That's when he started drinking again. And using coke. To numb the pain."

A sip of cappuccino. Then: "The coke wasn't a problem, to tell you the truth. It made him a relaxed person. We had good conversations, when he had used the stuff. The real problem was alcohol. He drank so much, it wasn't funny anymore. And most of the time it was hard liquor. It turned him into a monster. When drunk, he did the most ridiculous things, like pissing in a chest of drawers, in the middle of the night. Or in a vase. Of course, once sober again he denied everything. Which almost always lead to him having a tantrum. Under these circumstances, his standard threat was to leave us. And that's what he eventually did, in Turkey."

At this very moment, he doesn't drink anymore. For the simple reason that he can't lift a glass anymore – let alone a bottle. But he still uses certain substances. "No coke anymore," says Veronika. "He doesn't have enough strength to snort it. It's cannabis oil, nowadays. I put a few drops on his tongue and that's it. The stuff doesn't get you stoned, but it's very soothing. You can sleep better, it gives you a better appetite and, on top of that, it helps against drooling and spasticity."

Another sip. And a smile.

"But you know how Nando is. He always wants more, more, more."

She tells about the time she came back from the supermarket. "Guess what? There's Nando on the floor, hallucinating, surrounded by empty bottles. Turned out he drank 'em all! While you are only allowed to have four drops a day. Drops! Not bottles! But that's Nando for you. Doesn't know how to dose things. On the other hand: by now he should realise that he can't do it on his own anymore. I mean: I even have to assist him when he goes to the loo!"

She tells me she doesn't know what to do now. "I think I'll stay here, for a while. With my mother. I don't even know where Nando is at this moment. He doesn't answer my messages anymore. Have you heard anything from him, recently?"

"Nothing."

"Why is he doing this? We are here to support him! He must realise that! Hopefully he will come to his senses pretty soon. So I can tell Bella where her father is. She doesn't understand why he didn't show up on her birthday. Try to explain that to a child!"

JULY 1, 2015: **Indulgence**

I need to know what's going on inside Fernando's head. So I make an appointment with Bram Bakker, a well-known Dutch psychiatrist whose best friend suffers from MND. Bakker wants to say a lot of things – he is very talkative – but in a way he can't. He can't say anything about somebody who isn't his own patient. And if Fernando were his patient, there is always such a thing as professional secrecy.

"So I can never say he is hooked," says Bakker. "That's public diagnostics, as they call it. A mortal sin, in the medical world. Completely not done. Even when it's obvious."

So Bakker has to say things like 'there is a possibility that this and this person consumes more alcohol than desirable.' Or, in the case of someone like George Best: "He probably died due to certain physical complications caused by his way of life."

As newspapers have written so much about Fernando, it's obvious to Bakker that at least he can call him 'the Dutch George Best.' Or 'the Dutch Paul Gascoigne.' "I can also use the word 'indulgence', as that is not something medical. And it's there for everyone to see. It's when people don't know their limits. In fact, no limits at all. Do you know what they say at the AA? One beer is too much, a thousand are not enough."

Bakker is not surprised that Fernando has hit the bottle again. "MND is all about control. The lack of control. So in a way what Veronika says is right. MND does affect the brain. The problem is: the medical world nowadays is very specialised. A special discipline for every disease. MND has to do with the muscles, so it's a job for neurologists. But a neurologist only looks at the muscles, not at the brains. Here, we do miss the old fashioned nerve doctor. He was a neurologist AND a psychiatrist. He would have noticed any changes to the brains as well as to the muscles."

He continues: "And don't underestimate what a diagnosis like this does to a person. Especially because you don't know what caused the disease. It's not like a chain smoker who gets lung cancer. We don't understand MND. Nobody does. That's why it feels so unfair."

"The strange thing," I say to him, "is that Fernando likes to joke about his condition."

"Not that strange, Vincent. There are Jews who make jokes about World War Two and concentration camps. Somehow that makes them stronger."

"And how about the effect the coke has on him? Normally people get fucked up, but Fernando gets quiet and even reasonable, after a few toots."

"That is because he is quite, er, vivid by nature. In his case the blow works as Ritalin. Calms him down. It's like an ingredient. Like pepper on a plate of pasta. A bit of pepper spices things up, makes it better. As long as you don't overdo it."

JULY 7, 2015: **Sepp Blatter (5)**

An e-mail from Sepp Blatter – again. The man who just has been re-elected as big boss of the FIFA writes: "My dear Fernando, I wish you continued strength in the battle that you are so bravely fighting."

JULY 27, 2015: **Spanish sun**

"Wait a second..." Veronika says, before wiping a drop of sweat from Fernando's forehead.

We are in the Spanish tourist town of Benidorm and it is scorching hot. But it's the kind of temperature that Fernando loves.

We're here to celebrate his 39th birthday. He, me, Veronika and Isabella, who just flew in from Russia, and a big bunch of Rangers fans, who will gather tonight at The Ibrox Bar on Calle de Lepanto.

He said it before: the heat does him good. Thanks to the sun, he can speak a bit better – and his fingers feel less crooked, or so he says. And, maybe even more important, he is on speaking terms with the entire world again.

I try to listen to him, but in all honesty I have great difficulties in understanding him. And his fingers are just as crooked as they were six months ago.

"Of course," he mumbles. "Sun doesn't beat MND. It just makes the patient feeling a bit better."

What he wants to say, is: he prefers Spain to Belgium. That's why he didn't hesitate when his Scottish friend Victor invited him to his house in the hills above Alicante, a few weeks ago.

It's not a holiday, he wants to let me know. It's also some kind of revalidation, although he knows (and accepted the fact) that he will never be the old Fernando again.

"You should have been dead by now," I say to him, recalling the words of the doctors, right after the diagnosis.

"I know," he says, with a smile. "The trick is not to think about death and instead, concentrate on life. Sounds a bit naïve, but it works. I'm still here."

Hence his new project: his own clothing brand. It's gonna be called FR2. Fernando Ricksen number two, in case you didn't get it yet.

"Lots of things to do," he says, gulping down a small bottle of mineral water. And no, he doesn't know when he gets back to Maaseik. He very much prefers Spain. "I've got a swimming pool here. Ideal!"

AUGUST 18, 2015: **Honking**

"You did WHÁT???"

"I drove to Urmond."

"On your own?"

"Yes."

"From Spain??"

"Yes. In one go."

"But how??"

"By car."

"And you were driving??"

"Yeah, no problem. Only a few difficulties at the French toll gates. I couldn't reach the pay machine, from the driver's seat. And of course I couldn't step out either. So everybody behind me was honking."

"And what happened next?"

"People at the toll gate were very friendly and they helped me."

"Okay. Anyway, I see you tomorrow. It's at the Van der Valk hotel in Urmond, right?"

"Yes, but can you already do me a favour?"

"Of course. What is it?"

"I can hardly make myself clear here. It's that voice. So can you please call the hotel reception and ask them to bring me something to eat? I am starving."

"And what is it that you want?"

"Potato puree."

"No problem. But hey, Fernando: you're nuts!"

"What's new?"

AUGUST 19, 2015: **Bruises**

"Fernando!!"

"Hi Vincent."

"Your face! It's covered in bruises! What happened man?"

"I fell. In the shower."

"So it's obvious that you can't stay on your own. Not at your house in Maaseik, but not in a hotel either!"

"I know. That's why I contacted my mother. As from today I'm gonna stay at her place."

SEPTEMBER 20, 2015: **Elgin**

Of course she said yes! Rachael Brown, a 19 year old Scottish sports therapy student, was asked to work as Sports Therapist at a Rangers Legends match in Elgin, and she didn't hesitate one second. It's a charity thing – i.e. collecting money for MND Scotland – and at the same time it would be a chance to meet her idol, Fernando Ricksen. In her earlier teens, a large photo of Fernando had pride of place on her bedroom wall. Now? Pictures of her memories with Fernando are on show with even more pride.

We're having a bite to eat at The 1629 restaurant, a centuries-old pub in Lossiemouth and Rachael is all smiles. Although: "It was a difficult moment when I saw Fernando for the first time. I mean, I knew he was sick, but seeing first-hand how much MND had affected him was soul destroying. Then I saw his courageous, infectious smile and it really gripped me."

Bobby Petta has different problems. After all, it must be quite difficult for a former Celtic player to share a table with a bunch of ex-rivals from the blue corner. But today isn't about animosity. Today is about friendship and respect. So Petta can easily rub shoulders with the likes of Marco Negri, Andy Goram, Marvin Andrews, Michael Mols, Derek Ferguson, Alex Rae, Jonatan Johansson, Dave McPherson, Charlie Miller, Colin Hendry, Regi Blinker, Enrico Annoni, Tom Boyd and Joe Miller. And, more important, he can hug Fernando.

"On beforehand I was nervous," he confesses. "How to react when I see him in the state he is? But Fernando doesn't want you to feel sorry for him. That doesn't help him at all. So we sat down and chatted, like old friends. With a laugh or two."

Petta, from Rotterdam, loves Scotland. "Look at the sun!" he says and indeed, outside the pub a few rays are visible. Nevertheless it's a rainy day. Ah, Scotland...

Petta talks, Fernando listens. And of course the conversation is about The Old Firm of 2000. The one in which Fernando was substituted, after just 22 minutes. After which he kicked in one of Parkhead's dressing room doors. It was probably Petta's best game ever.

I decide to do a bit of shit stirring. "Didn't Pierre van Hooijdonk say something about that game?"

Of course I know the answer already.

"Yeah," grins Petta. "It was around the Holland game against Andorra, for which we were both selected. He said to me: 'Please turn around, Bobby. Otherwise Fernando won't recognise you.' That was quite funny."

"Or wasn't it, Fernando?"

He nods and smiles. And doesn't want to talk about that Old Firm too much. It still hurts, the 6-2 defeat. And no, he couldn't stop Bobby that afternoon. The bastard was way, way too fast for him.

"It's all about preparation," says Petta. "I'd analysed Fernando, in the weeks prior to the game. So I knew what his weak points were."

"What were his weak points?" I ask.

"He used to fall for every feint," knows Bobby. "So I did a few dummies. And off I went."

Fernando nods.

"That's why I loved playing against you. You never knew what I was going to do."

Fernando nods again, this time a bit slower.

"And in the next Old Firm he was sent off," Petta continues. "But those two games toughened hum up. Made him stronger. And look: in the end he became team captain and Player of the

Year. Quite impressive."

Petta isn't the roadrunner of yore anymore. Anyone who watches him in the testimonial in Elgin, this afternoon, can see that. Sitting next to a smiling Rachael, Fernando witnesses how his former team mates are struggling to get to the ball before the opponent does. But who cares. It's a fantastic afternoon.

And then there is Rebecca Mennie, the Rangers fan who decided to run half a marathon for Fernando. Not only did she complete her private sponsor run, she also gave birth to a son (not at the same time – ed.) which she named after her idol. And she can prove it.

"Look, here's the birth certificate! 'Mason John Fernando Stephen, born July 26 2015, 7.23 PM, at the Maternity Hospital in Aberdeen.' Do you think Fernando wants to sign it, Vincent?"

Is the Pope Catholic?

Oops, wrong metaphor!

But as much as Fernando tries, his signature on the certificate is a disaster. At this stage, he can hardly hold a pen anymore, let alone write with it. Nevertheless, the scribble makes Rebecca happy. At least she didn't come all the way from Aberdeen for nothing.

As she kisses him, I notice that I can't keep my eyes off his totally crooked fingers. It is going *very* fast now! I now understand why he told me he will stop sending me text messages by phone. He simply can't use the tiny keys anymore.

It's e-mailing, from now on.

OCTOBER 6, 2015: **Brainwashed**

I can still understand Fernando (a bit) when he speaks – but I am about the only one left. People who haven't spoken to him since he got ill, are facing enormous difficulties. An interview with him is hardly possible. That's why Sieb Oostindie, reporter for leading Dutch newspaper *De Telegraaf*, asked me for assistance.

We decide to meet in Heerlen, where Fernando's mother lives. And Fernando himself, not to forget. With Veronika and Isabella still in Russia and him being unable to take care of himself, he went back to the parental nest. He even resides in his old boy's room. It's on the first floor of the humble abode and climbing the stairs is very, very difficult for him. But he refuses to use a chairlift, as he wants to train his sick muscles at all cost.

However, last week he was too tired to go upstairs. No strength left – and nobody around to help him. So he stayed on the ground floor to sleep on the sofa. But then, in the middle of the night, he fell off it. Because by now his sense of balance is totally fucked too.

"I think I spent over three hours on the floor," he tells Oostindie, at the start of the interview.

"But at least I know how to fall by now," he adds. "Stiff as a shelf. Just like earlier this year, at Ibrox."

"How about a wheelchair?" asks Oostindie.

"That's not me," answers Fernando. And: "It's too early for that."

"It depends how he wakes up," says Fernando's mother Anneke, from whom he is no longer estranged. "When he wakes up all by himself, he is ready to conquer the world, more or less. But when I have to wake him up, it's a different story. If that's the case, he is totally upset."

Which isn't difficult to understand. Fernando IS upset. And that's because he has been separated from Veronika and Isabella for too long. Yes, he is going to visit them for a few days, at the end of the month. But the extra difficulty is: Anneke and Veronika don't like each other very much. So a choice for Anneke is a choice against Veronika – and the other way around.

"They both think the other one isn't treating me well enough. But that's rubbish. They both do it their own way. They both care about me."

"But at the moment he is here," says Anneke, decisively. "That was the deal. If he can't live on his own anymore, he would come here."

"After all, this is home," adds Fernando. "Home is where your mother is."

"That's not the Fernando we know," says Oostindie. "As a player, you were totally self-centred, egoistic. You didn't care about other people at all."

"I had to be," is the answer. "I wanted to reach the top. One can only do that by being egoistic. But now I'm a different person. I've changed a lot – and not just physically. I'm more honest to myself and to others. And I realise how empty, how fake the world of football is. My excesses were nothing but an escape."

"He has always been a strong boy," says Anneke. "But he has been used by the football world. He turned into someone I didn't recognise anymore. And the enormous amounts of cash didn't do him any good either. It's like, one way or another, he has been brainwashed in that world, a world that isn't ours. Look around you, this is where Fernando came from. We are very ordinary people. The money and the attention changed him, that's for sure. And now he feels sorry for it, I can see it in his eyes. I am sure he wants to tell me all kinds of things, but he simply isn't capable of that anymore. He got trapped inside his own body."

OCTOBER 14, 2015: **RTL Late Night**

Humberto Tan is a Dutch tv presenter (of Surinam descent, so the name Tan is hilarious – ed.). His talk show is called *RTL Late Night*. And at this very moment, he can't believe his ears.

"WHAT is it you're gonna do??"

"Down the pub," is my answer, "for a few beers."

"With Fernando??"

"Of course!"

It's about an hour after the show. We were invited to chat about our glossy *FERNANDO*, which will be released tomorrow. The studio from where the show is broadcasted is on Amsterdam's vibrant Rembrandtplein and none of us wants to go home yet. The official presentation is scheduled for next afternoon, in the sleepy village of Velserbroek, so there's plenty of time to down a few. And not just beer. Like the evening before, Fernando wants to visit [famous coffeeshop] The Bulldog too, to smoke a joint. Moments like these are basically what he lives for, nowadays.

So here we are, a little bit later, in the aptly named Club Amsterdamned, drinking that yellow stuff with froth on it. And yes, Fernando still drinks 'like a child', with the glass clamped between his wrists, but he doesn't give a toss. It's beer – and the taste is delicious.

Hey, what do you expect Fernando Ricksen is drinking in a pub? Milk??

OCTOBER 15, 2015: **Magazine**

We are in Velserbroek (between Beverwijk and Haarlem, not very far from IJmuiden, with its ferry to Newcastle), where *FERNANDO* (the magazine) is going to be launched. An interviewer from [tv station] Powned has seen it already and is very excited about the feature we did on the pole dancers of Maximus, a strip joint in Saint Petersburg. The photos, shot by the brilliant Goffe Struiksma, are indeed mouth watering.

"Do you know each of them personally?" the drooling reporter wants to know.

"I used to," says Fernando. "But this is the new breed."

Attending the ceremony are, among others, Arthur Numan (who, after all, is from nearby Heemskerk), tattoo king Henk Schiffmacher (best buddy of, to name a few, the Red Hot Chili

Peppers) and good old Willem van Hanegem. And once again Van Hanegem, who officially receives the first copy of the mag, can't hold his tears. "But I'm not ashamed of it," he says, one tissue later. "I've known Fernando for quite a few years now. Back in the day, I was convinced he would turn out to be one of the best defenders in the world. So strong, so determined. And to see him as he is now... It hurts, it really does."

OCTOBER 16, 2015: **Rehab**

FERNANDO is a Dutch glossy, so it's full of Dutch subjects. There is, for instance, a feature on former speed skater Jan Ykema, who successfully kicked his coke and, er, speed habit. There are interviews with football legends Giovanni van Bronckhorst, Frank de Boer, Phillip Cocu, Rafael van der Vaart and four of Holland's most delicious women (tv presenter Miljuschka Witzenhausen, model Femke Weijenburg, actress/presenter Katja Schuurman and saxophone player Candy Dulfer, who performed and recorded with none other than Prince himself). From other countries, the magazine contains, for instance, a feature on the Belfast of George Best and an interview with Belgian writer Herman Brusselmans, the self-proclaimed 'best pussy eater in Europe' (therefore we should call him a cunnilinguist). And there is an article about the rehabilitation clinic where Fernando stayed for a while. It's the private hospital we know from the very first lines (no pun intended!) of *Fighting Spirit*, the book.

The article in the magazine, headlined THE LAST STRAW, reads as follows:

This must be it. Welcome to Hampshire's green and pleasant acres! Surrounded by golf courses as smooth as billiards tables, there is this old, majestic Victorian castle. Its merlons are mirrored in the ancient building's pompous pond. Next to it, a wide range of expensive cars, like a BMW Coupé and a Range Rover Sports. Of course, as we are not dealing with a normal clinic here. This is detoxification-in-style!

This is for the upper-upper market, the place where the rich and famous - whether they sing, act or kick a football to earn their daily jewellery – come to get their act together. 'Champneys Forest Mere Health Resort' boasts the sign with the golden frame, that is located near the entrance. Of course it does. You don't welcome world famous rock stars and soccer players with a piece of wood saying 'Rehab', do you? A bit of class, please. And discretion.

So this must be it. This must be the place where you can, er, dry out with Kate Moss and share a bowl of soup – lentil, not goat's head – with Rolling Stones guitarist Ron Wood. If you're lucky, you may even enjoy a game of hand ball with Diego Maradona. Okay, you go cold turkey here and that hurts. But at least there are a few interesting people to share your pain with. And it's better crying in a posh place than in a dump.

"Clinic??" The woman at reception sends her eyebrows towards the ceiling. "Oh no, we're most certainly not a clinic, gentlemen! This is a hotel. The clinic is behind this building. They're our

neighbours. Just follow the small forest path..."

Sounds even more exclusive! But as we slide through the mud to reach our final destination, we are slightly disappointed, to put it mildly. Because what we see, are two old cottages and a more-than-average Ford mini-van. This must be wrong, we say to each other. This so-called Crouch House can't be the place where, since 2003, lots and lots of famous FA players have been treated for their addiction to booze, dope, gambling and porn.

"Oh yes, it is!" laughs Julian Keeling. And: "What did you expect? It's back to basics here. The guys who come here have been pampered enough in their everyday-life. Besides: this is not a holiday resort!"

As the psychotherapist shows us the rest of the place, we sober up ourselves – just by looking at its interior. This is so, er, normal. The furniture comes from Sweden. More precisely: from that big store that wants you to mount each table and chest of drawers yourself. We see a completely worn out dishwashing brush in a modest mug. And we hear the prizefighter aircrafts descending for nearby Gatwick. Down to earth – in more than one way!

"This here," Julian explains, "is a rehab cocoon. Four clients have to spend 26 days with each other. Those are the rules. In those 26 days, we turn into a little happy – and at times not so happy – family. We, the therapists, are the parents. They, the clients, are the children. And all of us behave accordingly."

Crouch House is part of The Sporting Chance Foundation, which was founded by Arsenal ace slash addict Tony Adams. He even spent four months in prison, after he'd jumped into his Sierra Cosworth, rat-arsed.

"A lot of players," says Adams, "are scared to admit the fact that they are addicted. They think it's bad for their careers. At least it's a lot easier for them to get in touch with us. It stays within their own secret little world, so to say, the world of football. It's tailor-made treatment here. Unique? Not really. There's even a special rehab for London Transport employees!"

In the absence of Tony Adams, Julian Keeling and James West run the clinic. A clinic, that once welcomed Fernando Ricksen. "How is he?" asks West. "Fernando is one of the nicest persons I've met here – and I mean it!"

Keeling and West are no strangers to substance abuse themselves. "From my 19th up until my 33rd I have used about everything," says Keeling, who combined his drug intake with a job as a magazine editor. "Booze, horse, coke, speed, you name it!" Dope-crazy James even ended up behind bars, a period that eventually changed his life. "I'm clean for about a quarter of a century now," he smiles. Being an ex-junkie, he sees things that 'normal' people don't notice. "Sometimes, as I watch a television interview with a football player, I recognise things. Body language, the way the guy looks out of his eyes. More than once I have thought: you should visit our clinic, pal!" Still, lots of footballers are masters of disguise, when it comes to hiding their intake problems. James: "We even had a crackhead who played for a League One-team. I mean: crack! And still presenting himself as a professional athlete. Quite impressive, I must say."

Crouch House doesn't open its doors just for Premier League and League One celebs. Amateur and semi-professional football players are welcome too. Julian: "Star players in lesser known competitions feel the same kind of pressure. They have to deal with the same things. It's just that they don't have to read it in the tabloids, when they played a crappy match. They hear it in the local Tesco. It's on a much smaller scale, but as I said: it's the same kind of pressure."

Julian thinks the 'glory' days of binge drinking in British football are over. "A few years ago you were The Man when you drank at least ten pints in a row. It's not like that anymore. Players are more aware of their health." Tony Adams: "No beer no, but there are a lot of French players now who don't hesitate to down a few bottles of Beaujolais on a night out."

Still, core business in the Crouch House isn't alcohol abuse anymore. "It's gambling," according to James and Julian. "More and more guys become addicted to that. And to porn, we have to add." As Julian walks out to greet four new clients, he lights a cigarette. "No, I never gave up that habit," he says, shaking hands with the brand new, heavily tattooed Crouch House inhabitants. The quartet doesn't look sad or depressed at all. On the contrary: it's almost like they are on holiday.

"They are here on a voluntary basis," says Julian. "And most of them know each other. They're in this together, so shame goes out of the window." James, a little less light hearted: "This is literally their Last Chance Saloon. Either they sober up, or the wife leaves them. Or they get fired. Or they die. It's really that serious. We are not some kind of boot camp, where a player can get fit for a Champions League match. Those guys are sick – and they need to be cured."

Like Fernando, who ended up at the clinic after an ill-fated trip to South Africa with Glasgow Rangers (read the shocking details in Fighting Spirit *– ed.). And, we dare to ask, that other notorious sponge, Paul Gascoigne?*

"Yes," James says, "Gazza has been here. I used to call him The Dustbin, as he literally consumes everything, whether he drinks, snorts or pops it. Tragic, because he is such a nice guy. We had lots of laughs with him, as he is funny as fuck!"

Once in a while, he still drops by, just to say hello. Most recently he was staying at the Champneys Forest Mere Health Resort. For free, as its owner likes to be seen with famous football players. "And there he was, on the forest path, in his Champneys Forest bath robe. Brilliant." As we keep chatting, the clinic's own private doctor arrives with the medicines, predominantly sleeping pills. They are much needed as, according to James, Julian and Tony, the first night in rehab can be 'frightening'.

What follows after that first night, is a strict regime of yoga, massage, talks, health food and more talks. Due to that regime, many broken lives have been glued together again. Still, Tony Adams has his own method. "I have a picture of me going berserk during a match. Every time I feel tempted to have a sip of the wrong stuff, I look at that picture and I say: no! I never, ever want to be like that again."

NOVEMBER 29, 2015: **George Best**

I receive an app from Fernando. It's a photo of him, posing in front of a George Best mural. Together with Stan Gordon and

Victor Morgan he went to Belfast, for a meet & greet. The three went by boat – which they almost missed. Typically Fernando.

George Best, the original bad boy of football... It's not a coincidence that *FERNANDO* contains a story about him. Reporter Michiel Blijboom went on a so-called George Best Tour. This is what he wrote about it:

Windsor Park. Belfast. I'm sliding through the shit like George Best through the defence of Northampton (February 7, 1970: Northampton Town – Manchester United 2-8, Best scored six times). Dog shit, to be precise.

"It's a pity the gate is closed," says Bobby Cosgrove, leaning with his meatloaf-sized arms on the steering wheel of his car. While I try to keep my balance, Torvill and Dean-style, Bobby tells me what he intended to show me. Turns out he wanted me to have a look at the pitch where George Best scored Northern Ireland's most famous goal EVER. One that people still talk about, in Belfast's many watering holes. It was the 15th of May, 1971. Northern Ireland were facing England, here at Windsor Park. England had Gordon Banks, probably its best goalkeeper ever. It was less than a year after Banks made THAT save against Pele, at the World Cup in Mexico. A true legend he was. But George Best didn't give a, well, 'the-stuff-I-had-under-my-shoe' about legends or reputations. And he was cocky, our Beatle-coiffed Belfast Boy. So when Banksy was about to kick the ball to the other half of the pitch, Bestie simply put his boot in front of him – thus capturing the ball. And before Banks knew what had happened, Best had scored. As simple as that. Too bad that the

referee spoiled the party, by disallowing the goal. But who cares? Best still scores with it nowadays, in the pubs of Belfast. Well, it beats talking about politics or the Eurovision Song Contest, doesn't it?

Bobby Cosgrove would have loved to show me the goalmouth where Banks and Best clashed. But the stadium is closed. Instead, I slither through fifty shades of brown until I reach a brick wall, which is part of a railway bridge. By painting life-size murals on it, artistic football fans have transformed it into a shrine. Immortalised are goalkeeper Pat Jennings, Billy Bingham and somebody who looks like Danny Blanchflower. Plus George Best, of course, sporting the colours of his once-beloved Manchester United. It's great to see how a nation can honour its sporting heroes. Such a pity that, in their own way, dogs give a shit too!

Back in the car we are heading for Queens University. No need to have a look at road signs, as Cosgrove, who looks like he's just swallowed a beach ball, is taking this route for the umpteenth time now. Not that it ever gets boring, by the way. Oh no, he loves showing foreigners the Belfast of his youth, a youth he spent with a boy called George Best. Back in the day, at Nettlefield Primary School, they were class mates. Played football together, had fun. Most of the time they had to use a tennis ball for that, but on one occasion they were lucky enough to have a real football. Okay, it was a leaky one, but after stuffing it with old newspapers nobody cared about that anymore. And certainly Cosgrove couldn't tell the difference, as he hardly touched the damn thing. "George was constantly in possession of the ball," he remembers, "even as a little kid. You simply couldn't take it off him. He was a genius, a born footballer. Nobody had to teach him anything."

As we drive through the streets of South-Belfast, Cosgrove hands me a little present: a bookmark from the George Best Foundation. A percentage of the money that the George Best Tour generates, is donated to the aforementioned organisation. "They do something for liver diseases or so," he mumbles. By now, the entire car smells of poo. But we don't stop. In fact, we don't even halt to have a look at Queens University, the place we were heading for.

"It was in 2001 that George received an honorary degree here," my tour guide says, as we leave the beautiful building behind us. "He was extremely proud of it. But then: he deserved it. He was very intelligent, you know, had an IQ of 147. Some people say he could have gotten more out of life." Sharp turn to the right. "But I ask you, in capitals: HOW MUCH MORE?? The guy has had seven Miss Worlds! Seven!! I haven't even had one Miss Belfast!" I believe him.

By now, the George Best Tour has reached East-Belfast. Donard Street, more to the point, where young George and his parents lived with his grandparents, shortly after the war. It was in this street, says Cosgrove, that the famous picture of a juvenile George Best, juggling with a way-too-big ball, was taken. It's a remarkable pic indeed, as the toddler already has the posture of a professional football player. But thank God that, despite his IQ of 147, the pint-sized dribbler couldn't read yet - as there's a sign on the wall that says: 'NO BALL GAMES.'

And off we go again. To the Nettlefield Primary School this time, the place where Cosgrove & Best learnt to read and write.

The former stops the car and crawls out of it. As I follow him, he walks in a straight line towards the gate. Closed. Cosgrove sighs. Then, he sticks his forefinger through the gate. I can't help it, but this morning's breakfast sausage springs to mind. "See that piece of grass?" Yes, I do. "That's where George and I wanted to play football. But the school didn't allow us to do so. The grass was reserved for cricket games – and cricket games only." I wait for the punchline. No punchline.

As we make our way back to the car, I quickly check the sole of my shoe. Yes, it's still there. On we go. Left, right, left – and then we are face to face (sort of) with the biggest mural of a football player I've ever seen, both in reality and in my dreams. It's a massive painting of George Best Superstar, complete with blowing hair that looks like a crown of thorns. "My favourite," says Cosgrove, "'cos it's in black and white. After George died, people laid down scarves of Celtic and Glasgow Rangers, at this very spot. Catholics and Protestants, united in grief. It's unique, unique..." he says, as he staggers back to his vehicle.

We're heading for Burren Way, a completely anonymous little street. But hey, next to the door at number 18, there's a sign – although I can't read what it says. And it stays that way, as it turns out that my tour guide has promised the residents that he will never enter their garden. So we just have to guess. It seems that the Best family have lived here. George's send-off even started here. So hey, historical ground! Too bad we can't tread it. "Very impressing," I say to Cosgrove, grabbing for a handkerchief to hide my Pinocchio-nose.

Cosgrove, unimpressed: "Now take a picture of THAT!" 'THAT' is a blind wall. "Just do it," he says, "then I'll explain what you have photographed. I do as he orders. Back in the car: "There used to be a grocer on those premises. George was allowed to use it as a dressing room, when he was playing for Cregagh Boys Club." The old Cregagh turf is still there, partly shadowed by a block of enormous flat buildings. One of them sports a massive mural of George in the national kit of his beloved Northern Ireland. I want to get a bit closer, but Cosgrove warns me. "It's a swamp over there! You will disappear in it from your feet up to your knees!"

That would solve the problem of my smelly shoe!

But Cosgrove is already back in the car. Time for the grand final (already). We're about to meet George Best himself! Well, his remains, actually, at Roselawn Cemetary. As Belfast isn't exactly a metropolis, we arrive at the churchyard within minutes from the near-swamp experience. "This," Bobby Cosgrove warns me, "is going to be shocking!"

And there we go, cracking on the gravel path like Paul Temple inside your transistor radio. As we pass hundreds of people who reside 'on the wrong side of the grass', we're dribbling closer and closer to our ultimate goal: George Best's grave. "It's gonna be shocking," Cosgrove says, once again. "Shocking, because people have high hopes when they come here to visit his tomb. They think our best ever footballer is buried in a huge, towering monument. Marble, gold, enormous statues of angels, the lot. Well, er, in fact... this is it..." My eyes follow the little breakfast sausage. He is right. It's not much. Grave number 5295 has a simple, black stone. On it, the names of Angie Best and her 'dear son' George.

Two victims of that nasty old devil called King Alcohol. Yes, Angie was an alcoholic too. So there was basically no way that her dear son could have escaped his faith. It was in the genes, so to say. Irish from Scottish descent – not really an environment to enjoy a nice pint of milk! So when he was ignoring the NO BALL GAMES sign in Donard Street, all those moons ago, the toddler was not just destined to be a fantastic footballer, but also one hell of a boozer. Both careers were inevitable. Hitting the bar in the evening, trying to shoot under it on Saturday afternoon, so to say.

"I think I've found you a genius," were the now legendary words with which Manchester United talent scout Bob Bishop contacted his boss Matt Busby, way back in 1961. Seven years later the genius would win the European Cup. The real cup: the one with the big ears. Due to his popularity and flowering follicles he was baptised 'the fifth Beatle'. He would spend most of his millions to booze and birds. The rest, he squandered. Now that's what I call a genius! Yet, all that's left of him is resting under a simple, black tombstone. Next to the grave of the Lunn family. Sad? Not half as sad as what Cosgrove is telling me next. Turns out that his son lays here too. "He was sixteen, when he stepped out. It was the night before Christmas. I don't think I'll ever get over it. But I have to keep trying. Life goes on – unfortunately."

As we walk back to the car, I curse myself for making such a big fuss out of a little bit of dog poo under my shoe.

"Next: Stormont!" yells Cosgrove. So there is an encore after all. Stormont, AKA the Northern Ireland's Parliament Buildings, is where George had his funeral service. Hundreds of thousands of

people gathered along the road to Stormont, to pay their resp... "HEY, WHAT'S THAT??" Cosgrove stops the car. And puts it into reverse, until we reach a tiny little road sign, saying: 'George Best Statue.' My guide hasn't got a clue. It's the first time he sees it. And he is curious.

"Maybe it's something nice for my tour," he says, before we go off road. As we bump up and down like Katie Price on a date, we approach an old sawmill. We jump out of the car and regret it immediately: the soaked soil sucks us like, well, Katie on that same night out. We bravely plough towards the wooden work place, where we are greeted by its foreman, in his green wellies and matching chequered cap. We ask him if we can have a look at the statue. "It's not finished yet," the man answers – but that doesn't exculpate him. For what he is showing us in his shed, is something that Pygmees in Central Africa may find impressing, but is an insult to the late, great George Best. The massive wooden piece of occupational therapy sports arms that reach to the ground, also because it has legs that even Henri de Toulouse-Lautrec would find insulting. And the face... My God, the face! If you want to see a Northern Irishman in its features, then it's former Undertones singer Feargal Sharkey – after he headbutted the Dublin to Belfast intercity, at full speed.

Five thousand pounds, is what the artist wants to have for this carefully mistreated tree trunk. But for that money, he promises to paint it in club colours of your choice. We tell him that we will think about it.

"If this guy wants to be part of my George Best Tour,*" says Cosgrove, as he puts his mud-stained foot on the accelerator*

pedal, "he first has to make his premises accessible. Let's face it, I can't do this to my guests!"

We continue the promptly aborted route, until we reach Stormont. Well, its impressive gate, to be precise. The complex itself is featured on the horizon and looks like a sparkling sugar cube. "You can walk to it," says Cosgrove. "It will take you approximately half an hour." A quick calculation. All in all, that's more than sixty minutes which I can't spend in the places where one REALLY pays homage to Georgie Best: Belfast's incredibly cosy pubs. "Next time," I lie. Cosgrove doesn't object.

The next moment, we find ourselves on the highway. The next *next moment, we're alongside that highway. "Look, George Best Airport!" says Cosgrove. I look. And I see George Best Airport. I look again, this time at the guy next to me. He seems to be miles away, in a different galaxy. A different era, more to the point. For sure he's thinking about that little boy from Belfast, the boy he tried to play football with, behind the fence of the Nettlefield Primary School. The boy who would always have the tennis ball. And, in later years, the beauty queens. The boy who, eventually, would have a complete airport named after him.*

"That's the end of our tour," says Cosgrove, thus breaking the short silence. Then, as he starts the car: "Interested in a Van Morrison Tour *too? I used to know Van as well, you see." I tell him I'm not doing it, for the simple reason that it can't get any better than this. 'Cos this was already... Best.*

DECEMBER 12, 2015: **Broken hand**

Back to Fernando, who fell on the floor – again. During a visit to the training ground of Rangers, this time. It's serious: he broke his left hand.

"Shit," he tells me in an e-mail from Scotland. And: "Please put something on Twitter, so my fans won't be too worried."

A few minutes later, his followers can read: "My hand may be broken, but my willpower isn't!"

2016:
The Frustration

JANUARY 11, 2016: **Cristiano Ronaldo**

'PING!' goes my phone.

'PING!'

'PING!'

'PING!'

'PING!'

'PING!'

'PING!'

Seven times. Enough for seven photos, sent by Fernando's Scottish friend Victor Morgan, with whom he went to this year's Golden Ball ceremony in Zürich, Switzerland. I look at my screen and I see:

Fernando with Lionel Messi. The latter has his arm around our boy.

Fernando with Neymar.

Fernando with Daniel Alves.

Fernando with Paul Pogba.

Fernando with Cristiano Ronaldo.

Fernando with Cristiano Ronaldo.

Fernando with Cristiano Ronaldo.

Yep, three pictures with the Portuguese superstar, who even kisses him on the head.

"Friends for life," says Fernando, via Victor. Oh, and there's an invitation from Ronaldo too. To come to Madrid, one day.

FEBRUARY 12, 2016: **Ink**

An article about Fernando's love for tattoos, under the headline THE NEEDLE HAS LANDED:

Rock 'n Roll *is the name of Fernando's favourite tattoo shop. It suits him, as his life has been rock 'n roll to the max. Compared to* Fighting Spirit, *the book about his first 39 years, Keith Richards' autobiography is like something that was written by Enid Blyton. Well, sort of. Rock 'n Roll is situated in Glasgow's Watson Street and inside, Fernando feels like a kid in a candy store. "The sound of the needle," he grins, "is what it's all about. It's like music to my ears."*

He certainly isn't the only (ex-)footballer who likes the odd gallon of ink being pumped into his body. On the contrary: it's easier to find a steak in a vegetarian restaurant than a modern football player without tats. "It's an addiction," says Fernando. "Once you have one, you want to have more. And more. And more. I must have collected over a hundred illustrations now."

Nowadays, even really big stars are hooked on ink. Fernando: "Even the greatest of them all, Lionel Messi. I don't think many people expected that. And look at my fellow countrymen Wesley Sneijder and Gregory van der Wiel. I think they look super cool!" Asked about his favourite tattoo, Fernando shrugs his shoulders. "I have too many of them to answer that question, mate. I have the Rangers crest on my calf, the name of my daughter Isabella on my chest, the name of my wife Veronika on my tummy... and about 120 other illustrations, ha ha. The one between my shoulder blades is a good one too. It was done by Henk Schiffmacher (AKA Hanky Panky, who also put his signature tats on people like Robbie Williams, Willy DeVille, Kurt Cobain, Lemmy Kilmister and every single Red Hot Chili Pepper, minus the dead one – ed.). I'm really proud of that one. Henk is a legend. The tattoo he did on me says Vivere Militare Est. *In proper English:* Living Is Fighting. *It matches the* I am a warrior with fighting spirit, I will never give up and never surrender *on my belly. That's my motto. Especially now, in this phase of my life."*

Glasgow is where it all started. "It was in my second season at Rangers," he recollects. "One tattoo, just for fun. A dragon, on my arm." A normal dragon? Hey, this is Fernando, so: "An enormous one." What followed, very soon, was a collection of stars, roses and compasses. Unfortunately, from that moment on, some people treated him like he was a chav. "Just because of a little bit of ink! Ridiculous! I have a friend who is a cop. He is not allowed to have visible tattoos. Why not? If he catches crooks, who cares what's on his arms? Why can't he have an image in his neck?"

Like, for instance, Fernando himself. The very moment we enter Rock 'n Roll for a bit of, er, shopping, he tells [Polish tattoo artist] Marek Hali that he wants a big owl in his neck. The alternative was a huge portrait of his daughter, on his back, but ten hours in the same position would have been too demanding for the MND patient.

"An owl symbolises wisdom," says Fernando. "Should've done that much earlier. Because I've done a lot of stupid things." Like? "Like having the name of my ex-wife tattooed on my arm. It was

quite difficult to get rid of..."

...both the wife and the tattoo. We all know the story about the court case and stuff.

Five hours later, the owl is where it will stay from now on. And Fernando is more than happy with the result.

"I'm tired now," he says, "otherwise I would do the other side of my neck too. The tattoo shop is the one place where I can forget about my illness. Do you know how nice that is?"

A nice article, but with a bit of poetic freedom. No, a LOT of poetic freedom! Because at this stage, Fernando can't produce all those long sentences anymore.

More to the point: he can hardly speak.

MARCH 1, 2016: **Stubborn**

"Look," says Roy Knez, "that's where she found him."

We are in Nieuwstadt, north of Sittard, where Knez lives. He is a good friend of Fernando. In fact, Fernando and the returned Veronika, are living in his house now, as the landlord kicked the Ricksens out of their home in Maaseik. Knez points out where Fernando ended up, after falling down from a flight of stairs, with which he broke his hand, wrist, cheekbone and jaw, and on top of that cut his eyebrows and hurt one eye and an ear.

"Terrible," he says – and that's an understatement. But, on the other hand: "He could have broken his neck too."

He'd found it weird already, the fact that Veronika wanted to FaceTime him, while she knew he was having a work-related training in Kerkrade. "But as soon as I looked at my screen, I knew it was serious. There he was, lying in a puddle of blood."

As he tells me the whole story, I look at the mummy on his sofa. The *giggling* mummy, would you believe that?

"He wanted to leave the hospital immediately," says Veronika.

"Understandable," adds Knez, who is a policeman and who has seen quite a bit of blood and bruises in his life. "He likes it here. This, at the moment, is his home."

Knez didn't hesitate one second, when Fernando asked if he, Veronika and Isabelle could stay with the policeman and his girlfriend Mirthe. "Yes, it's the second time he asked me for this favour and no, I don't mind at all. That's what friends are for. You help one another if you can. But I'm glad that this time Veronika is here too. Because Fernando's condition is a lot worse than twelve months ago. Back then, he already couldn't have a shower, all by himself. But now he can't even eat on his own. Hell, he can't even get out of bed without our assistance!"

But, says Knez, the weaker Fernando gets, the more his admiration for him grows. "His perseverance is unheard of. This guy is... It's unbelievable."

He remembers a charity dinner in Glasgow, two years ago. "Fernando had his picture taken with the first person who asked for it. And with the second. And the third. Man, he went on and on and on... And there were a thousand or so people in the house! He simply didn't want to disappoint anybody."

"Of course not," mumbles the mummy.

"He went on until half pas one, night time. Typically Fernando."

He looks at the unfortunate former footballer on his couch and says: "I never have to ask him how he feels, because I know the answer already. It's always: yeah, fine!"

Veronika: "Like yesterday, at the hospital."

"Even then," sighs Knez. "It's just that..."

A gasp of air.

"He shouldn't be so stubborn all the time! Like when we were at AZ, that match against FC Dordrecht. When he went on the pitch at halftime, for about ten minutes. That was the idea. But after twenty minutes he was still there! They couldn't even start the second half because Mister Ricksen had some more hands to shake!"

The mummy chuckles.

"He'll never change," says Knez.

MAY 4, 2016: **Mobility scooter (1)**

"Time for a mobility scooter," he writes.

Finally, I think. Finally he realises that he can't go on like this.

MAY 8, 2016: **Mobility scooter (2)**

"I still have to get used to it," he says.

I stare at him – and at the enormous bandage on his forehead.

He asked me to come to his new apartment in Maaseik, where he now lives with Veronika and Isabella. And with his brand new mobility scooter.

"It's ideal," says Veronika. "So much easier to go into town now. He could even go on his own. It's just that he hasn't done it yet."

"Is he ashamed?" I ask.

"Oh no, no way! That's not the case. He is just a bit... How shall I say it?"

"Clumsy?"

"Exactly! He doesn't know how to handle the thing yet. So yesterday, when we went to the Designer Outlet in Roermond..."

She pauses.

"You know Nando, right? Always playing the part of the clown. Always wanting to be funny. So yesterday, in that big shop..."

She pours herself a glass of cola, takes a sip and sighs: "Full speed! Through the entire shop! With Bella on his lap!"

"Great fun!" yells Fernando in the background.

"Yeah, hilarious. Especially when you didn't know how to brake."

"Haha."

"Not funny! Vincent, he bumped into all kinds of products that were on display, crashed and fell out of his scooter!"

"Hahahaha!"

"STOP LAUGHING! So once again we had to call an ambulance."

"Yeah, well... Things happen."

"I was scared, you have no idea. Because once again he was covered in blood. So I said: for the time being, you are NOT going out on your own! First a bit of practice with that thing. In the living room!"

MAY 21, 2016: **Mobility scooter (3)**

The phone rings. It's Veronika.

"Not normal!" she shouts. "It's not fucking normal!!"

"What isn't normal?" I ask.

"You know where we just found Nando?"

"I have no idea."

"On the highway!"

"I beg your pardon?"

"On the fucking highway!!"

"Oh dear."

"On the hard shoulder. With his mobility scooter. He had left home because he was pissed off, for a change!"

"And?"

"When I found him, after a bit of searching, I immediately pulled the key out of the machine."

"And now?"

"Now he's home. Even more pissed off."

"That's a relief."

"But it's not normal, is it?"

"Not really."

"All things could have happened. A mobility scooter on the

fucking highway! It's never finished with this man! But I told you before: MND corrodes the brains as well. There is no other explanation!"

JULY 20, 2016: **Beard**

MND or not, Fernando still wants to look as good as possible. Hence his frequent visits to Hairplanet, a trendy barbershop in Sittard. Today is one of those days, where he sits in the hairdresser's chair to have his hair styled and his beard trimmed. Or, more to the point, he is lying in the chair, nowadays. With the barber's hands on his head – and a camera in his neck. This, because as from today New Earth Productions is filming him for a documentary. A real life soap, as they call it.

Today is an easy one for the cameraman, as Fernando just lays down and enjoys the treatment. He once told me that these are his favourite moments nowadays. Only at the barber's, he can relax.

He really, really needs this.

AUGUST 6, 2016: **Vulnerable**

"We had an agreement: we can film anytime and anywhere, or we stop!"

Ronald Top, producer of Fernando's real life soap, is displeased with Veronika's phone call that Fernando is 'too ill to cooperate today'. We are in the lobby of the Hotel RH Victoria in Benidorm, not far from The Ibrox Bar where Fernando once again made a triumphant appearance. But now he can't get out of his bed anymore. And he doesn't want Top to film that.

"Without scenes like this, the documentary has no value," he grumbles. "Yes, last night was great. But we can't film just that. There are two sides to the coin. The viewer has to see what an evening like that does to his body. Otherwise it's useless. I want to make an honest film. You do understand that, don't you?"

Yes, I do. As much as I understand that it's Fernando Ricksen we're dealing with. A man who does what he wants. Even now.

SEPTEMBER 29, 2016: **Katie Price (2)**

"I never had sex with that man."

It's Jordan again, doing her best Bill Clinton impersonation. Once again she labels Fernando's story as 'bullshit'. This time she does it at the launch of her umpteenth book. And hadn't Fernando been so sick, she would have sued him.

"The only bullshit comes out of her mouth," says Fernando as I tell him what she said to the tabloids. "And if she really thinks I am lying, she can sue me too. The fact that I am sick shouldn't make any difference."

OCTOBER 6, 2016: **KLM (1)**

Fernando has finally changed his rented house in Maaseik for his holiday home in Náquera, Spain. He bought it fifteen years ago, without a mortgage. Now, at least, he doesn't have to worry anymore whether he can pay the rent or not.

Unfortunately it also means that going up and down to Scotland has become more difficult for him. Yes, there are direct flights from Alicante to Glasgow and Edinburgh, but Alicante is a three-hour drive away. And by now, Fernando can hardly keep his neck up.

The alternative: flying from Valencia, which is basically around the corner. But from there, there are no direct flights to Scotland, which means that he has to change planes, halfway. Not ideal either, but a lot better. Especially because [Dutch airline] KLM knows him by now, so Fernando in turn knows what to expect.

Or so he did. But not anymore. Not today. Most of the time he flies on his own, as Russian Veronika never gets a visa for Great Britain, and it never led to major problems. Once again: until today. Because today, Fernando is denied boarding. The reason: he can't open and close the safety belt on his own. So three hours later, he is back in Náquera.

"Unbelievable," he writes to me. "Thought I was in a candid camera show. Can you please call KLM for me? I am finished for today. The stress has completely worn me out."

OCTOBER 7, 2016: **KLM (2)**

Once again Fernando finds himself in front of the KLM desk at Valencia airport. Once again they check his crooked fingers. Only this time they decide to let him on board, with excuses. He still can't handle the belt on his own, but KLM decides that a handicapped person simply should be helped, when needed. So Glasgow, here he comes!

Again.

OCTOBER 8, 2016: **Ties**

"Look at us!" jokes Victor Morgan. "As if we are going to a funeral!"

The location is his house in Hamilton and he just tied Fernando's shoe laces.

It may have been a joke, but at the same time it could have been true. Because the guys DO look like they are going to a funeral! But that is because tonight's dress code is black tie.

Tonight stands for: a big MND awareness gala at the DoubleTree by Hilton Hotel Glasgow Central. Celebs galore! Plus Nacho Novo and Alex Rae.

"It's all about dignity," says Victor. "Fernando wants to look as smart as possible – especially now, in his condition!"

And that's why Fernando looks the part, as his temporary wheelchair is pushed into the posh hotel, where over a thousand people have gathered. A thousand *Rangers* people, on top of that.

Among them, of course, Rebecca Mennie, mother of a baby she named after Fernando. "A name well picked," she says. "The little one is quite, er, temperamental."

Alex Rae knows what she means with that word. As the entire lounge starts singing "WE LOVE FERNANDO, WE DO! WE LOVE FERNANDO, WE DO! WE LOVE FERNANDO, WE DO! FEEEEEERNANDO WE LOVE YOU!" he tells us about the madman's habit to whack everyone with a newspaper, after arriving at Murray Park – in the morning! "But," adds Nacho Novo, "he is one of the funniest men I've ever met in my entire life. Maybe the funniest. And one hell of a player. Hard as a rock. Not one you want to face as an opponent."

To be a 100% sure that he will never, ever forget about him, the Spaniard came up with something. "Look," he says, as he drops his trousers to unveil quite a big tattoo on his leg. 'Fighting Spirit' it says, above two fists. And underneath: 'Fernando'.

"He is my friend," says Novo. "And I take him with me in my grave."

Fernando, in the meantime, is having a ball. It's just a pity that Cristiano Ronaldo couldn't make it tonight. He'd loved to be here, according to his agent Jorge Mendes, but he had 'different obligations'.

Bullshit? No at all! Because at the end of the evening, all of a sudden Mendes's face appears on the big screen. And out of the face comes an invitation on behalf of Cristiano Ronaldo. An invitation to visit the upcoming Champions League match Real Madrid v Legia Warsaw, as special guest of the Portuguese superstar.

"Fantastic..." mumbles Fernando, as he is put into his wheelchair to be taken back to Hamilton. A fitting end to a ceremony that wasn't even *close* to being a funeral!

OCTOBER 19, 2016: **Cristiano Ronaldo (2)**

No, he has never been to the Estadio Santiago Bernabéu in Madrid. But as he sits down in one of the white seats inside Cristiano Ronaldo's private VIP box, he immediately feels at ease.

Yes, he could have been here in 2008, when Zenit Saint Petersburg played Real Madrid, but a certain Fernando Ricksen wasn't part of Zenit's selection, back then. For obvious reasons. For being his temperamental self.

Biggest concern tonight is how to keep little Isabella quiet, for 90 long minutes – and more. Not because she doesn't like football. No, Bella, wearing a white tutu, is constantly jumping up and down because she wants to meet her big idol: Ronaldo.

"When are we going to see him?"

"I want to see Ronaldo!"

"Is he coming soon, Mommy?"

"Where is Ronaldo?"

"Have you seen Ronaldo already, Daddy?"

"How much more do we have to wait?"

"Is Ronaldo about to come?"

"Where is he??"

The wee ballet dancer has to wait until two minutes to midnight before she stands face to, er, knees with the Real Madrid ace. Who immediately starts cuddling her.

"That's a dream coming true!" says Veronika with a smile, bright enough to light the entire stadium.

Fernando, sitting in a wheelchair, gets a hug too. "Keep fighting," whispers Ronaldo in his ear. And just like in Zürich, it is followed by a kiss.

Fernando doesn't say anything. But I notice that his lips start trembling. Two minutes later, tears are running down his cheeks.

NOVEMBER 13, 2016: **Diego Maradona**

Is he coming or isn't he?

No he isn't.

After three days of uncertainty, Diego Maradona finally speaks to us from Dubai. He isn't coming to Brunssum. He isn't going to meet Fernando Ricksen. He simply isn't interested.

Despite the available Cohiba-cigars and, believe it or not, busty babes he won't show up in the small town in Limburg. Henk Butink, chairman of VV Heksenberg, the amateur football club where Maradona was to spend an hour or so, is furious. "A good footballer," he says to Fernando and everybody else who is gathered in a special party tent, "but I don't want to see him anymore. Ever!"

DECEMBER 14, 2016: **Tube feeding**

Fernando doesn't like hospitals. They make him feel depressed. That's why he wants to avoid them as much as possible. But by now, he doesn't have a choice anymore. Fact is: he can hardly eat. More and more often, food gets stuck in his throat. And he doesn't have enough strength left to swallow. It makes him cough and cough and cough. So it's time for tube feeding.

"A wise decision," says George Gorrie, neurologist at the Queen Elizabeth University Hospital in Glasgow, with whom Fernando made an appointment.

"It's all about the quality of life," explains Gorrie. "If you can't eat or drink, you're left with less and less energy. And on top of that you will get an almost constant headache. Plus you get more and more tired."

Gorrie advises a so-called PEG-tube, straight into the belly.

"Okay," says Fernando, after listening to the doctor. "Let's go for it."

"Blow!" shouts the nurse. "One more time: blow!"

It's the first of a series of tests. Fernando has a funnel in his mouth and a peg on his nose. And he has to blow, after which certain results are visible on a computer screen next to him. As the screen turns green, Fernando's face turns red.

"This was heavy..." he moans, a bit later. "So heavy... I am so tired now..."

He turns his face towards the window. Outside, it rains – for a change. He then turns towards me again.

"It's difficult now..." he sighs. "But I won't give up..."

I say nothing. I just think.

What a fighter.

2017: The Powerlessness

MARCH 26, 2017: **Fleetwood**

RANGERS ARE BACK IN EUROPE!!

Well, England that is. Fleetwood, to be precise, north of Blackpool. Beggars can't be choosers.

Due to the well-documented administration and liquidation, Rangers aren't allowed to compete in both Champions and Europa League. So every time a Gers team does play abroad, for whatever reason, they are followed by thousands of hungry (not to say thirsty) fans.

Like this weekend, when there is this testimonial for Fernando in the English coastal town of Fleetwood. Despite a three hour drive from Glasgow, over 10,000 Rangers supporters have turned up. Yes, that is less than the 250,000 who went to Manchester for the 2008 UEFA Cup Final against Fernando's Zenit Saint Petersburg but hey, give us a break!

"Unbelievable," mumbles Fernando in his room at the Hilton Hotel in Blackpool.

"Says everything about this club and the loyalty of its fans," adds Victor Morgan. "But Vincent, what the heck did you bring with you?"

"Just what he ordered," is my answer.

After row number Godknowshowmany Fernando has left Veronika once again and now crashes out on Victor's Scottish sofa. But he misses Dutch treats. Hence this wish list he mailed to me:

Autodrop Bosvruchtrode Cadillacs (2x)

Verkade Kids & Co. Prinses Aardbei (2x)

Conimex Noodles Thom Kha Kai (4x)
Kanjers Extra Grote Stroopwafels (2x)
Duyvis Pure & Natural Cashews Garlic Rosemary (4x)
Duo Penotti Hazelnootpasta (2x)
Timson Rinse Appelstroop (4x)

Victor is flabbergasted about the shopping list. And I am surprised about the way Fernando looks. Okay, he gets thinner and thinner. His arms are starting to bear resemblance to matchsticks. But despite that, there's still that twinkle in his eyes. He still hasn't given up. He still has that fighting spirit.

Very impressive.

"He'll never stop," says Stan Gordon, landlord of the Stonefield Tavern in Blantyre. He is the guy who is in charge of organising friendlies for The Rangers Legends. We met him in Elgin, earlier on.

Rustling up enough players for those matches is the easiest part. Everybody loves to play for The Legends, so building a good-enough team is about as easy as ordering two pints of lager and a packet of crisps at the Stonefield Tavern.

Today's Legends are, among others, Barry Ferguson, Charlie Miller, Gordon Durie, Ronald Waterreus, Pieter Huistra, Colin Hendry, Michael Ball, Marco Negri, Jörg Albertz, Marvin Andrews, Nacho Novo, Alex Rae, Arthur Numan and Michael Mols. They are faced with a bunch of English legends like Darren Anderton (Portsmouth, Tottenham Hotspur, Birmingham City, Wolverhampton Wanderers, AFC Bournemouth), Gavin McCann (Everton, Sunderland, Aston Villa, Bolton Wanderers) and Lee Hendrie (take a seat: Aston Villa, Stoke City, Sheffield United, Leicester City, Blackpool, Derby County, Brighton & Hove Albion, Bradford City, Daventry Town, Kidderminster Harriers, Chasetown, Redditch United, Tamworth, Corby Town, Highgate United, Basford United).

Least impressive name (although...): Alex Dick. He is not a former professional football player, but 'just' a Rangers nutter. Thanks to his 500 (!) pound donation, he is allowed to join The Rangers Legends. And he even scores! An afternoon never to forget, despite the 2-3 defeat.

But it's not just Dick's day (yes, that sounds funny). The evening belongs to 'cultural singer' Lynsey Glen, the blonde bombshell from Coatbridge. She is about to perform at Viva Blackpool, a well-known venue on Church Street in England's most vibrant seaside town. But she is nervous. Not for 999 of the persons who are going to hear her sing terrace classics like *Lads Who Follow Rangers* and *Every Other Saturday*. No, it's number 1000, Fernando Ricksen. "He has always been my favourite player, so it's a big honour to sing for him tonight."

She's gonna start with *Penny Arcade*, she says. Not because it is her favourite Rangers song – that is *A Trip To Ibrox* – but simply because it's a great song to start an evening with. "It sets the tone immediately," she says. "Hey step up and play each machine seemed to say / as I walked round and round the penny arcade / Just ring the bell on the big bagatelle / and you'll make all those coloured lights cascade / And music played / at the penny arcade / Yes it played and it played / played all the time / Roll up and spend your last dime!"

"Are you gonna do ABBA's *Fernando* too?" I want to know.

"Maybe," she answers. "I haven't planned it, to be honest."

The signature song could bring tears to Fernando's eyes. And that wouldn't be the first ones today. As he had forgotten to take his medicines this morning, he was crying his heart out while on the pitch. The pills work as anti depressants and have him under control. So when he forgets to take them, he collapses, emotionally. In fact, he cried so much that he is asleep now, in his hotel room.

Chris Mayhead, former security guy at Rangers: "When I saw him crying, I almost had to weep myself. It was heart breaking. He simply couldn't stop sobbing."

But tonight Fernando has got everything under control again. Although he must be emotional when he realises that not just the expected 1000 Rangers fans turned up, but an astonishing 1500! He is still a bit shaken though, vulnerable, so this time he won't have his photo taken with each and everyone in the crowd. That would simply be too tiring.

And there is Lynsey, the vocalist who is tonight's major attraction after Fernando himself. She's wearing a figure-hugging blue dress and sings her heart out. Unfortunately Fernando is too weak to sing with her. But he smiles at her as she points in his direction. In the meantime, the rest of the crowd is belting out.

"It's the blue, blue sea of Ibrox / It's the greatest sight that I have ever seen / It's the blue, blue sea of Ibrox / And it's part of every Rangers player's dream."

MARCH 27, 2017: **Massive beamer**

Rachael Brown was again delighted to join Fernando & the team as Sports Therapist for what was a truly memorable weekend, she says. "The entire weekend was just perfect from start to finish. It really epitomized how loved Fernando is and always will be loved."

The Friday night was her 21st birthday party. "Thankfully I don't drink so I was on the Irn Bru all evening and wide awake for the early drive to Blackpool on the Saturday morning. It's safe to say that I couldn't have wished for a better way to celebrate my birthday weekend."

The number of people that turned up to show their support for Fernando was absolutely fantastic, Rachael adds, the entire place was a sea of red, white, blue & his native orange. "As a young Rangers fan growing up, I would watch my heroes from the stands, usually with my Dad Dave. So, for me personally, to go from being a little girl in a crowd of 50,000 at Ibrox, to working and building friendships with my idols, who include me as 'part of the team', is just a dream come true."

Rachael will never forget running on the pitch at Fleetwood to treat Colin Hendry who had just received a body blow to the ribs. "I could hear 'We want physio, we want physio!' being chanted from the stands. As I ran on, Lee Hendrie fell backwards pretending he was injured and needed medical attention too, which gave everyone a laugh!"

"And I remember having a massive beamer as I walked off, then Arthur Numan gave me a hug and said 'Rach! They love you, just give them a wave!'. After the match, we walked around the pitch with Fernando. You could really feel the emotion in the stadium, it was a powerful moment."

APRIL 24, 2017: **Trending topic**

Just like on October 30, 2013, the evening of Fernando's confession on live television, the man is trending topic on Twitter again. This, because his documentary, which was completed after all, is screened. It's almost as if the entire nation is watching. Minus one person: Fernando himself. "I know what's coming, so what's the point?"

MAY 10, 2017: **Stimuli**

We're on the veranda of Fernando's home in Náquera, Spain, and I have great difficulties understanding what he says. Yes, even I. It's become practically impossible to listen to him. Veronika may be the only person left who can decipher what he says. Very tragic indeed.

"He is so frustrated," says his wife on his behalf. "He can't do anything on his own anymore. He, who has always been the most independent person on earth. It really makes him angry. And all those people who want to shake hands with him. Can't they see that he doesn't have the strength for that anymore?"

She says that the situation leads to even more tensions in the

Ricksen household than before. "We would love to move on, but we can't. We're stuck in the mud. It's so incredibly... What are you saying Nando?"

He mumbles something in her direction.

Veronika: "He says that when he wakes up, he sometimes forgets he has MND. But then, when he tries to get out of bed..."

I nod.

"It has an enormous impact on me too," she continues. "I can't stay away from home for more than, let's say, two hours. He needs assistance with everything, including going to the toilet. So I have to be there for him when help is needed. Which is basically 24 hours per day."

I nod again.

"I also have to feed him. Constantly. Believe it or not: his muscles are still working, non stop, so he needs at least 4000 calories a day. Yes, that's an awful lot. Twice as much as a healthy man. Don't know why. I just know that without the calorie intake, he will collapse completely."

I take a sip of my coffee.

"And it has to be healthy food. That's why I only give him fresh stuff. I start each day by making a smoothie. A big one. One litre. Yes, that is enormous. But because it's thick and fluid at the same time, it is food that Nando can swallow without too many problems."

The tube he had attached in Glasgow, last December, is mostly being used for medicines, not so much for nutrition. Because the smooth stuff that Veronika prepares for him, is quite easy to gulp. "Dry bread is a different story," says Veronika.

"Especially the crust. But things like chocolate, pasta and sushi he can handle. Chopped sushi, of course. In little pieces."

Still, his muscles get weaker and weaker. Hence the weight loss of 15 kilograms, as muscles weigh more, the stronger they get. Apart from that, here under the Spanish sun, in his own environment, he isn't prone to new stimuli. Very important for an MND patient! He has to know what is going to happen, so he can be prepared. Surprises are not good for him. Therefore he didn't want to have a last-minute encounter with Dick Advocaat, when we visited PSV v Zenit Saint Petersburg, two years ago. The sudden shock would make him pull stupid faces, as he himself described it, back then. He needs to have time to prepare himself. A lot of time, actually. Had he known it a day in advance, it wouldn't have been a problem. As he does like Advocaat, his trainer from all those years ago.

So it is not that he can't enjoy things anymore. Oh no, he loves the occasional trip. It's one of the reasons why he hasn't thought about euthanasia yet. Also because, partly thanks to the medicines, he isn't in pain 24/7. He respects anyone who chooses to terminate his own life. But for him it's not an option. Not at this very moment.

He just hopes he lives long enough to be able to tell his daughter what's wrong with her father.

"Of course she does notice that Nando is different from other fathers," says Veronika. "But how do you explain MND to a 4 year old? Fact is, she only knows him as the sick person he is. And she learned to deal with it, in her own way. That's why she never asks Nando to lift her. 'Daddy is old', she says."

The fact that he is still alive, despite the 'four months to live' prediction from years ago, has to do with his background as a professional footballer, he thinks. Not just because of the physical aspects of being an athlete, but also thanks to the fact that he knows how to deal with disappointments. Because, as a football player, you win some and, yes, you lose some too!

"So you're not afraid of dying?" I ask him, via Veronika.

"Everybody has to die," she says, on behalf of him.

JUNE 21, 2017: **Doddie Weir**

And there's another one. After Jimmy Johnstone (football), Theodoor Doyer (field hockey), Stefano Borgonovo (football), Martijn Doldersum (football), Fons Bastijns (football), Jérôme Golmard (tennis), Carlos Matallanas (football), Krzysztof Nowak (football), Joost van der Westhuizen (rugby) and, of course, Fernando Ricksen (football) there's now Scottish rugby player Doddie Weir who tells the world that he has MND.

"Is there anything you want to say to Doddie?" I ask Fernando via e-mail.

"Try to do the normal, everyday things for as long as you can," he answers.

"That's the only way to deal with MND?"

"Yes."

SEPTEMBER 3, 2017: **Amsterdam City Swim**

You know Amsterdam, with its many canals. Not really the nicest water for a swim, to be honest. That is: under normal circumstances. But with thousands of swimmers at the same time it's quite okay – especially when it's for charity. And that is what the Amsterdam City Swim is all about: swimming for MND research. And this year, the starting gun is held by Fernando Ricksen.

"We are so pleased with his presence," says husky voiced Mari Carmen Oudendijk. The former sports presenter works as a volunteer for Amsterdam City Swim, an event that attracts lots of famous faces. This year we see, for instance, triple Olympic champion and former world record holder Pieter van den Hoogenband, former Rangers footballer Michael Mols, chubby singer René Froger, sports presenter Jan-Joost van Gangelen and Beau van Erven Dorens, the co-host who took over the famous *DWDD* interview with Fernando, all those years ago.

As a journalist, Mari Carmen Oudendijk knows how important the presence of famous people is, on an event like this. She likes to recall the 2012 edition of the swim event, its first. One of the contesters was no other than Queen Máxima of the Netherlands. "I've never seen so many photographers and camera crews in my life!" she laughs.

Today, Fernando is the event's main attraction. As I push his wheelchair towards the pontoon, we are surrounded by paparazzi. A few minutes later, I fire the starting shot. Yes, I do that. Fernando simply can't lift his arm, let alone with a heavy gun in his hand.

I wonder what people think. Maybe it's been months, or even years since they've seen him. For them, the image of the former footballer who can't even lift his head anymore, must be an enormous shock. So thin, so weak, so vulnerable...

That's why he draws more attention than the swimmers. That's why he is considered to be the real hero of the day. That's why someone like Ranomi Kromowidjojo, the beautiful triple Olympic champion (yes, just like Van den Hoogenband) wants to have her photo taken with him. Because, once again, Fernando Ricksen is the real hero at this year's edition of the Amsterdam City Swim.

As he lies on his bed in Dutch Design Hotel Artemis in the Amsterdam neighbourhood of Slotervaart, he still thinks about that particular word: hero. He thinks exactly the opposite: today's swimmers are the heroes. Not him.

Oh, and I ain't a hero either, according to Fernando. "That gun wasn't even loaded!"

Which is kinda true. I tried to fire a shot, nothing happened, the swimmers jumped into the canal and about ten seconds later I managed to produce a bit of a bang.

Anyway, talking about heroes: Ann Hamilton is one. The Scottish nurse came to Amsterdam to prepare Fernando's medicines. That is certainly somebody who deserves a deep bow.

A few hours later, we are inside Amsterdam's famous ArenA stadium, home of the mighty Ajax, to witness the World Cup qualification match between Holland and Bulgaria. Among the visitors: Pierre van Hooijdonk, of RBC Roosendaal, NAC Breda, Celtic, Nottingham Forest, Vitesse, Benfica, Feyenoord and Fenerbahçe fame. He now works for NOS, Holland's own BBC. Tonight he has to analyse the game.

Pierre waves at Fernando, who sadly can't wave back. I decide to walk towards him, to explain the current situation and to have a chat about the relation he had with him as a former opponent and team mate. After all, they both played for the Dutch national team at the same time. I ask him when the two met for the first time.

Pierre van Hooijdonk: "That must have been in the 1999-2000 season in Holland. I was playing for Vitesse, Fernando was defending the colours of AZ. He was only playing in our away game, in Alkmaar – and got one of the six yellow cards! I didn't have any physical contact with him during the match though. Peter Wijker was the guy who had to 'put a chain on me', as they say."

"Do you remember who scored the only goal in that game?"

"Yours truly, haha! A free kick, as per usual. It was my first season at Vitesse. Before that, I played for Celtic and Nottingham Forest. Fernando was about to go to Rangers. So we wouldn't face each other anymore, as opponents in a Dutch football match."

"What kind of player was he?"

"We were both fighters, battlers. Not necessarily the world's best football players, so to say. We really had to rely on our character. We had to work hard, give it the full 100%. No, better make that 110%. The big difference was: Fernando was immediately going for it, right from the very first whistle. He just went and went and went... until his tank was empty. I was a lot more, well, calculating. Fernando was also completely fearless. You really wished you had him in your own team, instead of in the opponents'. Anyway, that has happened too: I played three international games in the same Dutch squad as Fernando."

"What kind of guy is he? Or, actually, *was* he...?"

"It's fair to say that he had something... crazy-ish."

"Explain."

"Well, you wrote the book, so you should know, haha. Oh man, the episode in which he destroys two hotel doors... I was there, on that trip to Minsk. I also remember how he fell asleep on the coach, after demolishing those doors. Totally pissed. But that was Fernando for you. Unpredictable. He could get angry from one moment to the other. I remember a training camp in Hoenderloo. He was on the phone with his wife in Scotland. Man, it was as if he tried to scream to her WITHOUT the phone! Or the time when we had smuggled a few bottles of beer and some *bitterballen* (Dutch treat in the shape of a bollock, filled with scorching hot ragout – ed.) into our room. One of us broke those balls and put them under Fernando's blanket. The moment the ragout touched his toe, he went bonkers. Jumped out of bed and... smashed all the bottles to pieces! Needless to say that was the end of our secret little party."

"That was a Glaswegian reaction of him?"

"Quite possible. Glasgow toughens you up. It has happened

to me too. I have done things there that I do regret now, looking back. But it's the only way to survive in a volatile environment like Glasgow. The pure hatred between Celtic and Rangers doesn't leave you unaffected, as a player. Fernando was perfect for that city. A hard man, a warrior, in other words the kind of guy they really like over there. And after shagging Katie Price he REALLY became immortal!"

"You met him again in a UEFA Cup match."

"Yeah, that was the 2001-2002 competition. Which we won, with Feyenoord. Halfway to the final, we met Glasgow Rangers. Which, I can say now, we didn't like, for the simple reason that it was a damn good Rangers, with Stefan Klose, Tony Vidmar, Lorenzo Amoruso, Arthur Numan, Bert Konterman, Ronald de Boer, Andrej Kanchelskis, Barry Ferguson, Peter Løvenkrands, Claudio Caniggia, Michael Mols, Shota Arveladze, Tore André Flo and, of course, that Ricksen nutter. Who, by the way, was suspended when we played in Rotterdam."

"You didn't only kick around on the pitch itself. Before the match in Glasgow, you..."

"...mobilised all Celtic fans via the media. I simply had to use those powers. Everything was allowed, in my eyes. I mean: Rangers were the better team, so we really needed a bit of support when we played in Glasgow. I remember a young Rangers player who I almost kicked six feet under. That was terrible, something I am really ashamed of now. But we had to win that game and, as I said, Rangers were better. So we had to find other ways to beat them. Anyway, the green half of Glasgow loved it."

"And the other half hated you."

"As much as the green half hated Fernando. No, not true! Celtic fans hated Fernando more than Rangers fans hated me. Much more. Fernando is one of the most hated players in the history of Celtic."

"Nevertheless, they now are as sad about him being sick as anyone else. How and when did you find out about his MND?"

"I saw the re-run of the Dutch television show in which he announced it. It was... I was... Man, it's so sad."

"You didn't participate in the testimonial at Rangers."

"I couldn't make it, unfortunately. But I've seen some footage of it. Reminded me of the Stiliyan Petrov game, a former Celtic player who suffered from leukaemia. These are the moments that protestant fans cheer for a catholic player and catholic fans for a protestant player. And, after all, that's Glasgow too."

NOVEMBER 19, 2017: **Marco Negri**

Way back in 1997, Marco Negri maybe wasn't the best centre forward in Europe. But for sure he was the most productive! No less than 23 goals for Glasgow Rangers in his first ten games, that is quite an achievement. But the Italian striker never managed to break Dinamo Bucharest's Dudu Georgescu's European record of 47 goals in one season. Not because all of a sudden he couldn't kick a ball anymore. Not because he got suspended. No, it was because he got injured... during a game of squash with his team mate Sergio Porrini! The little ball went straight into his eye, like the big one went into the opponent's net for weeks in a row!

So Marco Negri knows what it is to deal with a big disappointment. That's why he is here tonight, for Fernando. Here, at The Ibrox Suite, for yet another Meet & Greet. After talking to the crowd, he gives Fernando a kiss on the forehead. Like Italians do.

2018:
The Worries

JANUARY 10, 2018: **Index finger**

How am I going to do this?

That's what I ask myself.

I have just pulled Fernando out of his wheelchair and while I have my arms around his thin waist, I wonder how to get him into my car, without bumping his head against the door frame. He, himself, doesn't have the strength anymore to cooperate. So I shove him inside, a bit like a ventriloquist's puppet.

Next question: how do I make him sit straight, with his head up? There's only 50 kilos of him left, but he's still a human being. And how do you handle that? I am not a professional, like Ann Hamilton, or a well-experienced caretaker, like Veronika. It looks so easy, the way they do it. And yet I am so clumsy. It's like ice skating. If you watch [eternal world champion] Sven Kramer doing it, you think: I can do that too! Until you try it and you hurt your back.

But then: what is a bit of back pain in comparison to what Fernando is experiencing? Not that he has much physical pain though. That's more or less killed by MND.

It's the mental pain that hurts. For instance: he is now wearing a diaper. That is humiliating. On top of that: it adds to the knowledge that he is losing this final battle. As much as he was determined to be the first person to beat MND, he realises that in reality, he won't be that person. It's only going downhill.

Today was meant to be the start of a happy trip to the Netherlands, as tomorrow his statue, near the stadium of

Fortuna, will be unveiled. But when I look sideways, during the trip from Eindhoven Airport to his old stomping ground, I don't see a happy man.

I see a very, very sad person.

His eyes are glazed.

I feel so sorry for him.

Was it the early flight from Valencia that wore him out? Quite possible. On the other hand, he always seemed to recover very fast from something like this, mentally. But now he doesn't. And that worries me.

I try to start a conversation, but the heavy rain outside makes chatting impossible. Besides, I wouldn't be able to understand him anyway.

Because it's over, when it comes to talking. Completely. He groans a bit, he mumbles a bit, he sighs a bit – but I haven't got a clue what he wants to say. And that worries me too.

A while later we are at the parking lot of the Van der Valk hotel in Urmond, where he will stay for the next three days, once again nursed by the wonderful Ann Hamilton. For basically the first time in the past few years I really feel uncomfortable. This is a surrealistic situation. Fernando tries to tell me something but I haven't got a clue what. Just like in the car. Even I, as one of the last persons, can't understand him anymore. It almost makes me feel guilty.

What I do next, is I grab his crooked index finger and lead it towards the keyboard of my phone. The moment I feel him pulling his muscle a bit, is the moment I know I have to push a button – with his finger. So very, very slowly I understand what he wanted to say.

A

B

N

A

M

R

O

That's 'ABN Amro', the name of a bank. Next:

P

I

N

'Pinnen' is the Dutch verb for: to get money out of an ATM. So there I have it: he wants to make a cash withdrawal!

He then gives me his pin code. And, after that, we produce another word:

C

H

O

C

O

L

A

T

E

An hour later, Fernando has spent 150 euros at Rousseau Chocolate, a specialised shop in the north of Sittard. And for the first time today I see a little smile on his face.

"Normally," says Mark van Bommel, seconds before he unveils Fernando's statue, together with Kevin Hofland, "one gets a statue when one is dead. But this is a different type of legend we are talking about. Fernando is a living legend."

It's all thanks to an initiative by Fortuna fans Geert Houben and Jimmy Nuchelmans, who asked fellow Fernando & Fortuna fanatics (that's a lot of F-words! – ed.) what would be the best way to honour Ricksen. Dieuwertje Mangeng, a long-time volunteer at Fortuna, explains: "There were three options. One: a tournament with AZ, Fortuna, Rangers and Zenit. Second: to name Fortuna's stadium after him. Third: a statue. Basically everybody chose option number three."

Now they had to find [the money for] a proper artist to do it. Because nobody wanted a disaster like that Cristiano Ronaldo thing on the island of Madeira. The assignment eventually went to Lia Krol (no relation to Ajax and Napoli legend Ruud Krol – ed.), who already made a fantastic sculpture of Dennis Bergkamp, which stands at the HQ of the Dutch FA.

It's not just a special day because of the statue. It's also the day of the evening on which Fortuna Sittard, number 1 in the Jupiler League (the Dutch First Divison – actually the second – which is named after a Belgian beer brand – ed.), can become 'periodekampioen' (champion of a certain period, as the First Division is chopped into different parts of which the winners end up in a play-off – ed.). "Funny," says Dieuwertje. "The last time Fortuna won a title was in 1995 – with Fernando. And now, 23 years later, he is here again. Hardly a coincidence."

As the statue is unveiled, a few minutes later, both Van Bommel and Ricksen start crying. It is, after all, a very emotional moment. They were football buddies, all those years ago. And, more important, they are friends for life.

"It's the biggest honour anyone can get," says Fernando, via his close pal Roy Knez. "From now on I can be here every single home game – and kick our players' asses!"

The crowd cheers. And does it again later that evening, as Fortuna wins the first *periodetitel* in its history. Thanks to Fernando? Yes, thanks to Fernando.

MARCH 21, 2018: **Not insured**

PING!

Veronika just sent me a photo. And I don't like that photo. I see a white van with the word AMBULANCIA. And the van got stuck in the traffic of Valencia.

I immediately call her, after which she explains what happened. It turns out that all of a sudden, Fernando couldn't breathe anymore. So she called an ambulance – which arrived after a whopping FOUR hours! And to make things worse: it didn't even contain a nurse. Just a driver!

"So Fernando is completely alone now, in that ambulance?"

"No, our neighbour is with him. I asked her to keep him company. But I think we're almost at the hospital now. Call you later!"

And that is exactly what she does, a few minutes before 8 PM. She has calmed down, after doctors sucked an enormous amount of phlegm out of Fernando's throat hole and trachea. Fernando himself is angry. More to the point: furious. Because he has to stay in hospital for God-knows-how-many-days. And also because it turned out that he isn't insured. So for every night at the clinic he has to pay 800 euros.

"Jesus Christ!" I say.

"Yes," she answers. "The only way I can take him home, is when I sign a document that discharges the hospital from any form of responsibility."

With Fernando being the stubborn person he is and knowing that they can't pay 800 euros a day, the inevitable happens: an hour later he is back where Veronika found him earlier on, gasping for air.

All that's left for her to do, is hoping that it won't happen again.

APRIL 16, 2018: **Doctor Deen**

Dokter Deen ('Doctor Deen') is a tv series situated on the Dutch island of Vlieland. It features top actress Monique van de Ven (of *Turkish Delight* fame – ed.) and lesser known faces like a certain Leopold Witte. Tonight, Witte is talking to *RTL Late Night* presenter Humberto Tan about his part in the series. He is accompanied by a blonde woman I know: Esther Kamphorst. Although she is introduced here as Esther Startman. She talks about Leopold Witte's part in the series, which is based on Erik Kamphorst, the former soldier who we met at the ADO Den Haag v PSV Eindhoven match in 2015.

"You played it exactly the way Erik was," she says to Witte.

Hang on, she said 'was'! Does that mean...?

Yes, on January 31, Erik passed away.

"Is it painful to see Leopold playing the part of your late husband?" asks Tan. "Or is it, in some way, comforting?"

"It's beautiful and terrible at the same time," the blonde masseuse answers. "And it's a pity that Erik died before he could see it. He was so much looking forward to it..."

JUNE 1, 2018: **Barbecue**

The 8th of May was supposed to be a day like all the others. A day of nursing, nursing, nursing. But then Dutch paper *De Telegraaf* popped up with the headline that Fernando Ricksen was about to die.

"The amount of phone calls I got..." says Veronika, on the veranda of their home in Náquera. "From Holland, from Scotland, from Russia... Everybody wanted to know if it was true. But it wasn't. Or, at least, not within the upcoming hours."

And, as she pushes him forward in his wheelchair: "This is not a dead man yet. On the contrary!"

And she smiles.

"I ain't gonna die within the next twenty years!" is Fernando's own belief.

"And why shouldn't that be true?" says Veronika, as she shows me the ramp they have made for the wheelchair. "Of course, it's very difficult. And it's gonna be even more difficult. A lot! But that doesn't mean there ain't any hope left. You do remember what the doctor said, right?"

I nod.

"Four months to live. Five at the most. But look at us now. It's five YEARS already, and Nando is still with us!"

He mumbles the name of professor Stephen Hawking, the world famous scientist, who worked on gravitational singularity theorems in the framework of general relativity and the theoretical prediction that black holes emit radiation. The guy who was the first to set out a theory of cosmology explained by a union of the general theory of relativity and quantum mechanics and who was a vigorous supporter of the many-worlds interpretation of those quantum mechanics. He just died, after having lived with MND for no less than half a century!

"And he probably didn't even die of MND, but of pneumonia," says Veronika.

In other words: Fernando Ricksen wants to be the new Stephen Hawking.

"And that's why we already started to plan my birthday party," says Fernando, via Veronika.

Once again the party will be held at The Ibrox Bar in Benidorm. Events like that, suck an enormous amount of energy out of him. At the same time, he really looks forward to them. And for Fernando, looking forward to something nice in the near future, is the best thing he can do.

Still, the newspaper article about his near-death had a dampening effect on his mood. Especially because lots of other papers (and websites) duplicated it, without checking whether it was true or not. At the same time: it felt good to know that so many people are worried about him. And it beats the anger, caused by certain fans of a certain Glaswegian club who want him to die as soon as possible. It's just a few of them, to be honest, but the things they write on social media are beyond human. Veronika: "Who are the real sick people here, Nando or them?"

To celebrate the fact that Fernando is still with us, Veronika has invited some friends for a barbecue. Among them a few women from Russia and Lithuania, who she met at Isabella's (international) school. "I'm so happy I've met them," she says, while cleaning tonight's capsicums. "Because of Nando's illness, my world has become smaller and smaller. I mean: I used to go to Spanish lessons and I did a lot of sports and gymnastics. But I can't do that anymore. I can't leave Nando alone for too long."

Yes, they can get a professional nurse. For two hours. Per month. "Two hours per DAY wouldn't even be enough!" she sighs. "So yes, it's heavy. Very heavy. Too heavy, to be honest. But Nando is my husband, the man I love. And if you love someone, you sacrifice yourself."

She starts each day at seven o'clock, with lifting Fernando out of bed. After that she washes him, dresses him and feeds him. Which takes, well, forever. Same for the visits to the toilet. "And in between, I have to take Bella to school. So before lunch,

I am already exhausted."

In the afternoon, Fernando sits in his wheelchair and watches tv. "And when I am out, to do a bit of shopping or to pick her up from school, I am completely stressed. Because I'm always scared that when I come home, Nando will be dead."

Just like in the morning, there is no time for relaxation in the afternoon. Once again she has to feed him, clean him, provide him with medicines... And she has to cheer him up too. The entire routine takes hours. Excluding the time she needs to do the gardening. "And no matter how tired I am, I can never go to bed before him."

More to the point: just before midnight she has to cook and feed him two steaks. Fuel for the declining muscle mass.

"Yes, it's crazy. But I have to do it. Somebody has to do it."

Anyway, tonight Veronika's female friends have already prepared the salad. And, er, I handle the barbecue. After all, that's a man's job.

Unfortunately I can't show Fernando how good I am at grilling big pieces of meat, because before the first juicy steak has hit the first plate, he is already asleep. The fuss around him has worn him out completely. We are not even going to wake him up for his daily portion of meat.

JULY 29, 2018: **Cake**

For the first time in four years, Fernando doesn't attend his own birthday party at The Ibrox Bar. Veronika has called the owners, John and Wilma Wallace, to say that he is too sick to come. Too weak. The latter can also be said of the enormous Rangers cake, that spent too many hours in the burning sun. Just after 9 PM, it collapses.

"A lost evening," says one onlooker.

SEPTEMBER 10, 2018: **Speech computer**

It's magic.

Science fiction!

I look at Fernando, who is sitting in his wheelchair, wearing a white football shirt and black shorts. Because yes, it's hot again, here in Náquera. He, himself, looks at a screen on a stand, right in front of him. His eyes sort of dance across the screen. And then I hear a female voice, saying: "For those who don't know me: I am Fernando Ricksen and I suffer from MND. Due to this illness, I am unable to speak. But this machine can speak on my behalf. It's the Tobii Dynavox 5."

It's the beginning of a little clip that we are about to put online. As Fernando wants everybody to know that thanks to Ton Krijnen of rdgKompagne, a company that provides communication possibilities for people with a handicap, his world has become a bit bigger again.

A few weeks ago, Krijnen read an article about Fernando and his current condition. And it made him think of [former field hockey player] Hansje Janssen, a woman who lives with MND for over ten years now. She benefits from an advanced computer that allows her to chat, type and skype, amongst many other things. "From what I've understood," Krijnen said, as he contacted us a few months ago, "Fernando still wants to do a lot of things. Well, the Tobii Dynavox 5 can be of great help then!"

Yes, Fernando still wants to do a lot of things. One of them was throwing the Tobii Dynavox 5 out of the window, shortly after it was installed for him. Because in the beginning he made one mistake after another – which pissed him off. One moment he blinked too much, the other he blinked too little. Or his eyes were at the wrong distance, meaning the entire installation had to be reset – which cost quite a bit of time. But after days and days of practice he now knows how to communicate via the Tobii. He can 'talk' and crack jokes. He can even play Isabella's favourite Disney movie. Extra bonus: as Veronika now immediately understands what he means, there are less struggles in the Ricksen household.

Today, Fernando feels so good that he can even answer a Rangers' fan's question about new manager Steven Gerrard. "Steven Gerrard certainly is the right man for the job. He is young, but at the same time he has a lot of experience as a leader. Just don't expect too much within the next few months. Give him a bit of time – and a lot of credit. I am sure he can turn Rangers into a club that not only dominates Scottish football, but European football too! He just needs the right support – from all of you. Like you supported me, in my first season at Rangers. Thanks to you I made it! Without you and your support we would never have had a Helicopter Sunday, arguably the best day in the history of the club. So I'd like to wish Steven Gerrard all the best for now and the near future. Bye for now and: see you on the 6th of October in Glasgow, for yet another meet & greet at Ibrox!"

An hour or so after we've put this clip on YouTube, it has scored half a million views already.

OCTOBER 7, 2018: **Dead?**

As I switch on my phone, shortly after landing at Schiphol Airport, I see that I have missed seventeen calls. All from Ann Hamilton. So it's obvious.

Fernando has died.

As I start shaking a bit, I think back at last night's events. The meet & greet in The Ibrox Suite started as a great event, with Fernando cracking one joke after the other. It had renowned gossip journalist Beverley Lyons doing what she does best. And the guy who did the auction threatened to show his cock, unless people would raise the bid on a signed shirt. But despite all the fun, I could see that Fernando, who was sitting next to me, was feeling worse by the minute. And around 10 PM he signed that he had to go. The constant coughing was causing too much pain. Besides, his throat was full of thick phlegm, which he couldn't get rid of.

A few hours prior to that, at the Holiday Inn in Hamilton, we already had to throw a glass of water into his face, as we feared he was about to collapse. And only last Friday, two days before the event, he had screamed for help. So he shouldn't have gone to Glasgow in the first place. But then, he didn't want to let his loyal fans down. They mean the world to him. So he went anyway. And that, eventually, cost him his life.

Or didn't it?

No, once again it's false alarm. Just like that time when he fell backwards on the Ibrox turf. Yes, says Ann, he's been taken to hospital, in Wishaw. But he is sort-of-alright. "He thinks he can fly back to Spain tomorrow. Personally, I am not too sure about that. At the same time, it's good to see that he's full of confidence again. So we'll see."

As I shove my phone back into my pocket, I think: my God Fernando, you are one hell of a fighter!

OCTOBER 9, 2018: **Exhausted (2)**

Fernando is still at the University Hospital in Wishaw. Of course he couldn't fly back to Spain. He is way, way too weak for that. "Just a few more days here, then back home," is what he writes to me. Still very optimistic. "I just did way too much, in the previous days. My muscles, the ones that still work, simply refused to continue. But tell anyone that I will continue doing those meet & greets. I'm not gonna slow down. Just a few days of rest and after that it's a completely new ball game! Just to let you know."

OCTOBER 17, 2018: **Palliative care**

Bad news from Scotland. Ann Hamilton tells me that she has spoken to a doctor, who decided that Fernando will get palliative care, as per direct. Because he won't live for very long anymore. Thing is: she hasn't told him yet, as he is still convinced that he can fly back to Spain next week. "But that is really out of the question."

"How long does he have left?" is what I want to know.

"Difficult to say. But we shouldn't think in terms of months anymore."

"But?"

"Weeks."

It hurts, that word.

"Sorry for bringing you this bad news, Vincent. Are you coming to Scotland, one last time? I already told Veronika that she should get her visa arranged – fast. Because I think it's very important that Fernando sees Isabella before he..."

She doesn't really need to finish the sentence.

OCTOBER 29, 2018: **Do's & Don'ts**

A message from Fernando.

"Tell Steven Gerrard to call me, if he needs me. I'm ready for a comeback at Rangers!"

Unbelievable. He's joking again. There is no ending to this guy's resilience.

Or is there?

Ann Hamilton had warned me already. "It's grandstanding. Please don't expect to meet the same Fernando that you saw a month ago. He is even skinnier than before. Every day they have to suck phlegm out of his throat. Be prepared. He is in very, very bad shape."

"Feeling relieved!" is what the computer voice says as I sit next to Fernando's bed. The cleaning of the throat has just happened, hence the remark. The cleansing itself is not much fun, he tells me. It must feel like a vacuum cleaner down your throat hole. "But it's better than choking," says the computer voice.

"What's the weather like in Holland?" he asks. "Does it rain as much as it does here?"

As I do my bit of small talk, I realise that I hardly look at him. Maybe it's too confronting. Tubes, lights, cords and hose pipes galore. Funnily enough I see a Celtic shirt too. On a chair, next to a Rangers one.

There is also a magnetic board, next to his bed. On it, a piece of paper with do's. And, remarkably, also don'ts.

I read:

DO'S

Always keep me upright.

May require suction.

Keep computer in front of me, red dots positioned in front of eye.

Ask yes & no questions.

Stand at bottom of bed when communicating.

Keep curtains closed at all times.

DON'TS

Lie me flat.

Ask too many questions at 1 time.

Look at computer when communicating.

Allow me to slide down bed.

I fully understand some of the Do's. Somebody who has difficulties in breathing, shouldn't be put flat. You even let him sleep sitting up. And somebody who just has a new computer with which he can make certain pre-programmed sentences shouldn't be showered with all kinds of (difficult) questions. No, one at a time. At his own pace. Leave him. Give the guy a break.

But the last Don't... I only got it when I thought about it on the train, back to Glasgow Central. All of a sudden I realised that I was guilty as fuck. I looked over his shoulder and completed his answers, while he was busy 'typing' with his eyes. Wrong! Humiliating! By doing that, I had robbed him from his last bit of freedom.

And of course it didn't help that some of my completions were wrong.

OCTOBER 30, 2018: **Mistaken identity**

As I walk through the streets of Wishaw, I bump into a shop called *The Neuk*. For a Dutchman this is hilarious, as 'Neuk' means 'Fuck'. So I take a photo of it. I'm convinced Fernando loves this. After all, he was in stitches yesterday, when he put his speech computer at 10, just as he was telling how he once shagged a girl opposite the Celtic ground. He loved the idea that it could shock the most prudish of the nurses.

But I'm not gonna show him the pic. Because I immediately see it's useless today. As Ann Hamilton has told me already, Fernando has good days and bad days. And today is a bad day. His hair is a mess and he looks so tired, so tired...

What a difference a day makes!

"I hardly slept," he says, via the computer. And: "I have something to say."

What he has to say, is already in the computer. He prepared it, so that he doesn't have to write it now, in my presence. It's a story about the previous night, 'the most terrible night of my life'.

He had to fight for his life. Without being able to move!

Some nurse, who shall remain unnamed, thought he was 'Peter'. The real Peter is situated in a room next to his. "It's enough for today, Peter!" the nurse said, before putting away his computer. And then... she put Fernando flat on his back!!!

And there was nothing he could do. He couldn't wave, he couldn't scream. He could just hope. Hope that somebody would find him in time. If not, this would be the end.

So there he was, flat on his back. Knowing that he was about to die, within... half an hour? An hour?

Two (!) hours later, a night nurse walked into his room. She immediately alarmed everybody. And saved the remainder of his life.

"I have never, ever been so scared," the computer says.

I ask him if he is furious.

"Why should I? They all do their best here." And: "People make mistakes." And, to top it off: "Is it still raining outside?"

OCTOBER 31, 2018: **Five years**

It's five years ago today. Five years since he officially heard that he has MND. In other words: 260 weeks.

1826 days.

43,824 hours.

And the worst is yet to come.

DECEMBER 8, 2018: **Harem**

No e-mails from Fernando for about a week now.

Is he too weak to do anything?

Or... worse?

No. The fact that he doesn't respond to my messages – including the one in which I tell him that Stephen Hillenburg, creator of SpongeBob SquarePants, has died of MND – is something technical.

He has been too fast with his computer. So fast that it got stuck. And nobody at the hospital knows how to reset or reboot it.

"So frustrating," said Ann, when she called me. "Not just for him, but for the nurses too. They haven't got a clue what to do!"

The word 'frustrating' springs to mind when I enter his hospital room again, six weeks after our last meeting. Without his computer he can't make himself clear AT ALL. He groans and he puffs, but he can't produce a single word. He now sports a set of cool sideburns though, that make him look a bit like cyclist Bradley Wiggins.

The good news is: I didn't come empty-handed. I bring him a brand new Tobii Dynavox 5, with the compliments of Ton Krijnen. Who, a wee bit later, gives us online instructions on how to install the thing. We even manage to add the browser version of WhatsApp!

This makes him a completely different person, mood-wise. He immediately is his own, witty self again. So when, a little bit later, I send him a photo of himself, surrounded by seven smiling nurses, his response is: "Ah, my harem!"

DECEMBER 15, 2018: **Proud**

After the umpteenth postcard of a Celtic fan, he tells me how great it is to see that all of a sudden sworn enemies stand shoulder to shoulder to show the same love and affection for him, the former Rangers thug. He wants to thank everybody, via a message on Twitter.

"You are both great, but together you are even greater. I feel very proud."

Half a million people like and share the tweet. Among them Celtic legends Stilijan Petrov and Chris Sutton.

"If this continues," I write to him, "you will win the Nobel Peace Prize."

"Here's hoping," he answers.

DECEMBER 18, 2018: **Hospice (1)**

He had shown me the photos already. The photos of a hospice. Because he knows that he can't stay at the hospital in Wishaw for much longer.

Of course, he prefers to fly back to Spain. To Isabella and to Veronika, who, by the way, still hasn't managed to arrange a visa that allows her to enter the UK.

But it's over. He can't fly anymore. Too risky.

It would kill him.

Yes, there was an offer from ambulance staff from the Netherlands, to pick him up in Scotland and then drive him home, via England, the Chunnel and France. But that would be utter madness. Besides, his Spanish home isn't really MND proof. There's just the ramp, that Veronika has added. But that's about it.

So he has to stay in Scotland, for the rest of his life. In a hospice.

"Nice room!" is what I hear from him, not much later. He mails me from St Andrew's Hospice in Airdrie. "It's almost like a suite! And they already installed the enormous tv set that I ordered last week. Are you coming soon? Would be nice to watch some football together!"

2019: The Resignation

JANUARY 11, 2019: **Hospice (2)**

When you get off the train at Airdrie's tiny little station, you walk straight into Broomknoll Street. You pass the Airdrie Working Men's Social Club, the Subway sandwich shop and a pub called The Robert Hamilton. Via Bank Street you reach South Bridge Street, from where you turn into Hallcraig Street. You then walk past the parking lot, cross Flowerhill Street, turn left and there it is: Henderson Street. Next to St Margaret's Catholic Church in the aforementioned street, on a hill, is the hospice where Fernando stays.

It's just a fifteen minute walk, but it feels like an enormous journey. Is it the slippery snow? Is it the fact that the streets are too steep for someone from the low lands? No, it's the fact that I don't know what to expect. What the atmosphere is in a hospice. Because, let's face it: a hospice is a place where people come to die, right?

But once again Fernando's eyes tell a different story. There is still (a lot of) life in the football legend! He grins, as he tells me, via the computer, that he bought lots of things for, believe it or not, a pleasant stay at the hospice. A gigantic television set, a Nespresso coffee machine, a sofa bed for Veronika and Isabella...

I grab the things he asked me to bring – a bottle of baby oil and two bottles of shampoo – and put them on his bedside table. After that, I ask him how he feels.

"Top."

I should have known! It's basically always 'top' with this man.

What a strong and positive human being!

"There's only one problem," he says.

I wait to take a sip of my Nespresso and stare at him. What could that problem be?

"One of the nurses is a Celtic fan."

I laugh. He does the same.

"But I'll work on that."

And he is serious! His idea is to have some photos of him, as captain of Glasgow Rangers, enlarged. On one of them he must be seen celebrating the Scottish championship.

"That'll teach her."

He still is very much a great ambassador of Rangers. And he still has a massive bond with his former team mates. Last Saturday some of them dropped by: Ronald de Boer, Marco Negri and Jörg Albertz.

"So nice," says Fernando via his computer. "All those memories... We had such a great time, back then."

Only problem: De Boer immediately put a photo of him and Fernando on Instagram, complete with the name and address of the hospice. So since then, everybody knows what we wanted to keep secret for a little while. The result: non stop phone calls. From fans, colleagues and journalists.

But we don't want a story in the press. Not yet. Or, more to the point: not without us staying in control. So what we decide to do: we compose an article ourselves and give that to *The Sun*. And then every other paper can pick and choose from that story.

JANUARY 13, 2019: **The Sun**

The headline is so big and heavy, you could smash a window with it.

Today, *The Sun* brings us, 'exclusively', an update on Fernando's situation. 'I'LL SPEND REST OF LIFE IN HOSPICE', the front page screams. The accompanying article is written by The Sun editor Ben Archibald. We read:

Stricken footie hero, 42 - who has been bravely fighting motor neurone disease for five years - has revealed the heartbreaking news that he will never leave Airdrie care unit.

The Rangers legend, 42, has been moved to St Andrew's Hospice in Airdrie after spending two months in hospital since taking unwell at a Gers tribute event.

And Ricksen - fighting MND - has revealed the heartbreaking news that he knows the rest of his life will be spent there - as he's not well enough to ever fly home to Spain.

He said: "I know I will stay in this hospice for the rest of my life. I have no other choice but to accept it."

Fernando told how it was his choice to be moved to St Andrew's - as it will improve his quality of life thanks to their caring staff.

He said: "I decided to visit here after being explained the options available to me by my doctors because I couldn't fly home due to lack of oxygen."

"And when I visited here it felt I came home."

"The staff are amazing and I know that this would be the place where I want to spend the rest of my life."

"I need professional care. I can't stay in Spain anymore. This will be where I spend the rest of my life."

"I've been here three weeks and I'm so happy. I care here."

"This place is incredible and the staff is fantastic. My room is like home - exactly want I wanted."

"It was depressing at times being in hospital - but it's not like that in a hospice. It feels like home."

Stricken Fernando has been battling motor neurone disease since October 2013 - after revealing his diagnosis live on Dutch telly.

He later moved to Valencia, Spain, with wife Veronika, 32, and daughter Isabella, six, because the warm weather helped his health battle.

But over time he lost the ability to perform basic tasks like tying his shoelaces, and was left so drained by the battle that he had to use a wheelchair to get about.

Last Summer he began using a Stephen Hakwing-style computer to speak to his family after the disease ravaged his voice.

And he was dramatically rushed to Wishaw General in October after taking unwell during a fans' bash at Ibrox.

He feared he had pneumonia after suffering chest pains at the event, before docs revealed he was suffering from exhaustion.

The scare saw him spend over two months in Wishaw General - before he moved in December to St Andrew's, which provides palliative care to people living with life-limiting illnesses.

Fernando - who spent six years at Rangers - added: "I didn't plan to stay here when I came over from Spain for one of the foundation nights but I was rushed to hospital with a very bad chest infection."

"I thought I would be out of hospital in a couple of days but a couple of days turned into a couple of weeks and I was there ten weeks."

"It was great on ward 6 of the hospital and the staff were amazing, but it was a busy hospital and I missed my own things."

"I was informed about other hospices by the staff but I already made the choice in my head to choose St Andrew's."

"It's always exciting to see if it is the right choice and the care is much better here for me. For example: there is a hoist for me, which we don't have in Spain."

"So I'm really happy and convinced that with the help of the hospice I will have the best time of my life."

He said one of the perks of the hospice is that he can get more regular visitors - as he still has many friends here from his time in Glasgow.

He was joined at the hospice last week by ex-teammates Ronald de Boer, 48, Marco Negri, 48, and Jörg Albertz, 47.

But he said the toughest part is being kept apart from wife Veronika and daughter Isabella.

He still FaceTimes the pair regularly, but Veronika hasn't been able to visit her ill hubby for nearly three months because of passport issues.

She is currently unable to fly over to Scotland, but is hoping to sort paperwork so they can be at his side shortly.

Fernando - shown yesterday in an Instagram snap chatting to Veronika over the phone - said: "I am happy here because all my friends are with me here in Scotland."

"Now for them it's easier to visit me. Easier than visiting me in Spain."

"The only thing that is very difficult for me is that I miss my wife and daughter. That was a hard decision for me to make to be without my family."

"Okay for myself it was the best option because I am feeling comfortable here and I get professional care 24/7, but it is very hard not being with my family anymore."

"But also for this the hospice has a solution. In my room there is a fold out couch that is specially for families."

"Now my family can come any time and stay with me the rest of my life."

Docs still have no idea how much longer frail Fernando still has to live.

He was originally given just months to live, but has already lived for over five years with the killer disease.

But despite facing up to living the rest of his life in the hospice, he's upbeat about the future.

He said: "I am not afraid or scared for the future."

FEBRUARY 8, 2019: **Steven Gerrard**

Today, Fernando is taken to Rangers' training ground, to be photographed with the current squad. Guys who want to win the Scottish cup – just like Fernando himself did, in 2003 and 2005. The moment the players see him, he gets a big round of applause. Just like in 2003, after he had grabbed those other cups: Katie Price's!

There is one big difference with sixteen years ago. Back then, he got fined by Alex McLeish, who had warned every single player not to get involved with the aforementioned sex bomb. This time, there is no fine. Of course there isn't. On the contrary: new manager Steven Gerrard comes up to him and embraces the stricken hero. "It's an honour for me to meet you," he even says.

FEBRUARY 21, 2019: **Pantaleon the Healer**

"One last question, Fernando."

The bedside interview with Stuart James of *The Guardian* is almost finished and there is just one little thing that the journalist wants to know.

"Is there something that I have to mention in the article at all cost?"

"Yes. Mention my wife please. That will make me score some points."

Talking about the wife: she is in Scotland. Finally. So after three long months the couple is finally reunited.

"You should have seen us last week," says Veronika. "We got so emotional, it took Nando a full day to recover from it. Three months... That is a very long period, Vincent! Especially for a little kid who misses her Daddy. She has been crying almost non stop. Yes, we FaceTimed a lot, but that ain't the same."

Because Isabella has to go to school in Spain, the two can't stay permanently. But Veronika's visa is valid for six months, so she at least she can come to Scotland quite often. "Like, er, every two weeks or so," she explains. "I just hope I can afford it. The closer we get to Summer, the more expensive flights to and from Spain will be. Don't think Nando's football pension, 1200 euros a month, will be enough."

But those sorrows are for later, signals Fernando, sporting the red clown's nose Isabella gave him. "I live by the day," his computer says. And: "I am not afraid of dying. Has to happen one day anyway."

I want to know if he believes in God. Ah, the things you ask someone with a clown's nose!

"Not really. What kind of God creates a disease like MND?"

Still, on top of his bed are two pictures of holy figures: Pantaleon the Healer and Saint Nicholas.

"A present from my mother. She bought it in Jerusalem." And then he says: "I get most strength from Bella. She is the main reason why I still fight."

"But what if..." I ask. "I mean... Is everything arranged for the funeral and stuff?"

"I hope so."

"And how do you want to be remembered?"

"Just as the guy I was. Nothing special."

"No?"

"Somebody who had fun. Somebody who couldn't behave himself – not even when suffering from MND!"

FEBRUARY 22, 2019: **Humiliating**

"Can you believe it? This man keeps going on. Despite his terrible disease."

Humberto Tan, him again, presents a football talk show called *VTBL*, and tonight Fernando is one of the subjects. His guests are heavily tattooed former Ajax and FC Twente player Theo Janssen and ex-Feyenoord figurehead John de Wolf. Tan just showed footage of yesterday's meet & greet at Tradeston Ex-Servicemen's Club in Glasgow.

"My hands are all wet," says De Wolf. "Goosebumps all over. But it's so humiliating to see what a disease like MND can do to a healthy guy."

"Yep," adds Janssen. "Very difficult to look at. I hope that, after a while, we will see the footballer Ricksen, when we think of him. Not just the patient."

Still, Fernando is not going to stay indoors. Yes, the whole world can see his decline. Because he wants to keep showing that very same world that he never surrenders. And in doing so, he may be an example to fellow patients. So it is more or less his task, his duty, to go out and show his determination. His braveness. His fighting spirit.

FEBRUARY 25, 2019: **Mongo**

I send him a mail because I want to show him something astonishing: a photo of a Celtic yob with a 'Ricksen is a mongo' tattoo on his upper leg. He even put it on Facebook, feeling very proud.

"What can I say?" is Fernando's answer.

"It's unbelievable, isn't it? *The Sun* already mailed me. They want a reaction."

"Better not. Too much honour for the guy. He has to live with it. What will he think when he looks at it tomorrow?"

"No idea. What do you think?"

"No idea either. But it's obvious who is the *real* patient."

MARCH 15, 2019: **Darth Vader**

"Look at me, I'm Darth Vader!" jokes Fernando, after nurses applied his oxygen mask.

Once again I am basically too scared, too embarrassed to look at him. I also realise: this is the next step towards the inevitable.

He didn't want it. He postponed it. But in the end, he didn't have a choice anymore.

There's only 40 kilos left of him, 6,30 in stones, and he wakes up with a headache basically every day. The lungs simply need help. Hence the mask, for at least ten hours a day.

"And?" I ask, after the nurse has left the room.

"So so," answers Darth Vader. "Very scary at first."

"Like... diving for the very first time?"

"Exactly. And I'm still frightened to sleep with it. It doesn't take away the fear of me never waking up."

MARCH 16, 2019: **Assassination attempt**

"You almost killed me, Vincent."

I am drenched in sweat. Because the awful truth is: I *did* almost kill him!

Fernando can laugh about what happened this afternoon. I can't. Not yet.

What happened: he asked me to bring him some Dutch sweets, just to change the taste in his mouth. He can't swallow food anymore, but sometimes he is in desperate need of a different flavour sensation. He then asks someone to put a treat on his tongue. Just for a few seconds, no more. It can be anything: a drop of ice cream, a crisp, a tiny piece of chocolate, or a liquorice candy. "My little moment of happiness," is how he calls it.

But today it went totally wrong.

On his request, I had been to [Dutch drugstore] Kruidvat to get him, among other things, some *Autodrop*, small liquorice candies in the shape of cars. But after two seconds on his tongue, the little car shot straight into his throat hole, as if Lewis Hamilton was driving it.

Normally, you then pat someone on the back. But in Fernando's case I couldn't do that. My hand would have gone straight through his fragile torso. But what instead? The poor guy was coughing, coughing, coughing, coughing, coughing, coughing, coughing, like a maniac. So I ran into the corridor, shouting for help. Luckily a nurse reacted quickly. And very, professionally. Incredibly calm, her fingers went into his mouth and got the little sweet out. No panic at all. God bless those people!

"This sometimes happens," Fernando then said, cool as ever. And: "That would have made one hell of a headline: BIOGRAPHER KILLS OWN SUBJECT."

I laugh, but more out of politeness.

Later on, the pay-off line of Autodrop's tv adverts springs to mind. The stuff is apparently 'too good', hence its slogan: IT SHOULD BE FORBIDDEN.

I totally agree.

APRIL 9, 2019: **Chris Eubank**

"Hi Fernando, how are things? I've just spoken to the Dutch FA. You will be on their upcoming 'Oranje Wall of Fame'.

"Top."

"How are you today?"

"Tired. Breathing costs a lot of energy. Oh, Chris Eubank just visited me."

"The boxing legend?"

"Yeah, that one. He had asked if he could visit me. But even without asking he would have been welcome. You simply don't refuse a person of his stature."

MAY 8, 2019: **Chair**

"Look!"

And that's what I do. I look at a photo of Fernando, sitting in a chair. With a red pillow in his neck. Sitting up, after having been in bed for three months in a row.

"But how...?"

"I just feel good."

"That's great, man!"

"Yeah, top."

"And more good news: you're on the Wall of Fame, at the Dutch FA's HQ in Zeist. You're hanging next to Frank de Boer."

"Cool."

MAY 14, 2019: **Bobby Petta**

Nineteen years later...

Nineteen years after that Old Firm at Parkhead, Bobby Petta revisits the man who, back then, couldn't get a grip on him. Playing against Fernando was fun, on that sunny day in the year 2000. But now, Petta can't laugh anymore. He is, in fact, close to crying, as he watches what's left of his former opponent.

"I was here a few days ago already," stammers Petta, "but they wouldn't let me in. They said you were asleep. Plus: I hadn't made an appointment."

"You can always come, Bobby. Always."

"Well, to be on the safe side, I made an appointment this

time. I told them that Fernando's Nemesis wants to see him."

"Yeah, funny." And: "I would have preferred Eros."

As the two split, two hours later, Fernando says: "You made my day, Bobby."

"No, Fernando," answers Bobby, wiping tears out of his eyes. "You made *my* day."

MAY 15, 2019: **Hospice (3)**

"What time shall I come, this Sunday?"

"Anything goes."

"Around 2 PM again?"

"No problem. I'll be here anyway."

MAY 17, 2019: **Pin-up**

The enlarged photos have arrived. Later than expected, but still, they're here, ready to be hung on the walls. One of them has a shirtless Fernando on it.

"I'll ask one of the nurses to unwrap that one," says cheeky Fernando, via his computer.

The idea is to cover the entire room in photos of Fernando. Photos of his glory days at Ibrox. And thus, half an hour later the room is like a museum. A Fernando Ricksen museum. The so-called topless picture got the most prominent spot.

"That's Helicopter Sunday," says [former Rangers security

guard] Chris Mayhead, pointing at one of the portraits. "I wasn't there. Too nervous. Went to *Star Wars III,* will you believe that? One of the biggest regrets of my life. As I saw the news [of Rangers winning the title] on my phone, I stormed out of the cinema. People must have hated me for it."

Rachael Brown, who is with him today, was 9 years old at the time. Nevertheless, she has fond memories of it. "I was at the airport with my parents, ready to fly to Spain. And then the news arrived. My Dad threw me up into the air with joy! He almost collapsed."

"Like what happened to me in 1995," says Chris. "I was part of Prince's security, when he was playing at the SECC. Girls galore! And man, they looked... amazing! Especially one. She really was like, er..."

"A groupie!" answers Fernando.

"Exactly. So I had to stop her. Couldn't allow her to go to Prince's hotel room. But guess what? It was his wife!! I felt so fucking embarrassed!"

We all laugh.

"Thank God Prince himself could laugh about it. And the next night, as we were in a club, he asked me if I could arrange some juicy chicks for him – and for the wife!"

I can see that Fernando is drooling. Literally, unfortunately.

"And that time with Meat Loaf, in 1995," Chris Mayhead continues. "Remember the floods? The gig got cancelled, so he asked me if I knew where to get a good curry."

Showbiz in one sentence!

"So we went to Mister Singh's. At least, that was the idea.

As halfway, he changed his mind. All of a sudden he wanted a kebab."

More showbiz!

"So we went to Sauchiehall Street instead. So there I was, in the middle of a Scottish street, in the pouring rain, next to a world famous artist who was stuffing himself with kebab. And not a single person recognised him!"

"We must have driven you up the wall then," says Fernando via his computer.

"Oh no, I loved you guys! I'll never forget the fact that each of you gave me 20 quid so that I could get my driver's license. Okay, one could say: what is 20 pounds for a football millionaire? But it's the thought that counts. The idea. And thanks to you lot I could pass my exam!"

He pauses. Then: "But yes, Fernando, you were a nutter. Just as much as Paul Gascoigne. Two incredibly good footballers who didn't know how to behave themselves. Hot-tempered too. I still remember how I had to step in when you had a fight with Sergio Porrini. I went for you first, as you were the strongest of the two. Remember that, Fernando?"

He nods.

"Dick Advocaat was furious," says Chris. "He said he would never put you in the line-up again. I then talked him out of it. Said that this showed how much passion was inside you. I told him: that's exactly the reason why Rangers need you. And in the end he agreed, so you were back in the team. I never told you this, did I?"

Fernando nods again. But this time with his eyes half closed.

He's getting tired, so we better leave the room. I say goodbye too, and just like any other time it feels weird. Because I never know if this could be a goodbye for ever.

Not that he wants to give up, oh no. He is still full of plans. He wants at least two more tattoos. The latest additions on his skin were done last February, when he asked Kirsty Lindsay of Kenny's House of Pain Tattoos in Hamilton, to come to the hospice. Besides that, he plans to attend at least one more meet & greet. Oh, and there are still ten (!) bags of Mentos Dessert Mints waiting for him.

Afterwards, Rachael says: "Fernando reminds me very much of my Mum, who we tragically lost to cancer in 2016. Before leaving the hospice I always say to Fernando: 'Stay strong & love you,' just as I used to say to my Mum. Both strong, beautiful people with real lion hearts."

As we are walking towards the exit, Chris recalls the incident at the training ground. "I grabbed him and, I swear, it was like holding a brick wall. And look at him now..."

He can't finish his sentence.

"I'm not feeling well either," he then says. "Lost my job."

"Fuck," I say.

"Yeah, but I'm not gonna bore him with that. After all, it's just work. You can't complain to a sick person about your work, can you? That would be ridiculous."

"I just keep going. It's nothing special. The people who take care of me do all the work."

Words from Fernando, about his stay at St Andrew's Hospice.

"He is right," says Deputy CEO Joy Farquharson. "Very well formulated by Fernando."

She has invited me for a chat, because she knows that there is a lot of misunderstanding about the phenomenon that is called hospice. "Most people think it's a place where only old and terminally ill people stay. But that isn't true. We also welcome people who require physical rehabilitation and help to manage difficult symptoms. Around 45 percent of the patients will go home again, after a while."

Indeed, that is something I didn't know either!

"So a hospice isn't all about death," she continues. "Of course, some patients die here. But as I said before: some will go home with their families."

"Anyway, we try to keep the quality of life up to high standards," adds her colleague Angela, who just arrived. "So we offer all kinds of therapies, more or less made to measure. Like music therapy, for instance. Or spiritual help."

The latter isn't really wanted by Fernando, Angela says. "But he loves it when our cleaning lady starts singing for him."

"And it doesn't matter that he has been a famous football player," says Joy Farquharson. "At St Andrew's, everyone is treated equally."

To keep the hospice going, 88,000 GBP is needed – per week

on top of funding received from the NHS. The money arrives via donations, fundraising, lotteries and charity shops. And of course there are the sponsored events, varying from kids who do voluntary work to people who raise money by climbing Tanzania's Kilimanjaro, to name just an example.

According to Farquharson, among those who raise money are a lot of (former) footballers. That might be true, as I remember what Arthur Numan once told me. Together with Michael Mols and their former Celtic rival Tom Boyd he once climbed Ben Navis, Britain's highest mountain.

"Fantastic," she says, reaching out for her cup of coffee. "And earlier this year we received no less than 9000 pounds from the Rangers Charity Foundation, being the result of an auction of football shirts."

Auctions, charity evenings, meets & greets... They are the kind of events Fernando is still living for. Pauline Glen still visits him at the hospice and she still wants him to attend the meetings she organises for him.

Farquharson starts laughing.

"Yes, that gives us the occasional headache."

"Like that tattoo!" adds Angela.

"Oh yes," says Farquharson. "We'd never seen anything like it. He just had a tattooist, here, on his bedside! It was something different, I can tell you. And a huge responsibility – for us! Like those meet & greets, outside of the hospice. What if something happens there? We are responsible for him!"

"At the same time: we can't stop him," says Angela.

Farquharson: "If there's something we really think would be

too risky for him to do or if we just can't facilitate it, we reason with him. And he understands that."

Angela: "Absolutely. And he never gets angry. More to the point: he is always very friendly. He always says 'perfect, thank you'. Always. And..."

She starts giggling.

"...just a few days ago, something nice happened. All of a sudden there was somebody at the door, with a big box of donuts. Turned out that Fernando had ordered them, online, from Tesco. For him it was another way of saying those two words: thank you."

JUNE 20, 2019: **Tutu**

Yesterday was Isabella's seventh birthday. And it was celebrated in great style. At the hospice in Scotland, with mother Veronika, father Fernando, balloons, cake and lots of presents.

"All Nando's work!" says Veronika, with a proud smile. "Many healthy fathers won't make that much of an effort!"

This is the kind of memories that, hopefully, will last forever, she continues. "Look at those two. The bond they have... Can I say something stupid? I sometimes envy Bella!"

It's, obviously, also due to the fact that Fernando always said yes when Veronika said no and always said no when Veronika said yes. "When I tell her that she has to go to bed, Nando tells her she doesn't. That kind of things made the two of them inseparable."

The fun they have together hasn't gone unnoticed. [Dutch radio reporter] Roos Oosterbaan looks at father and daughter and smiles. And it makes her feel better than a few minutes earlier, when she entered the room. Roos, herself invalid due to a spinal cord infarction, wasn't even sure whether there was a body under the blankets. Because yes, by now Fernando is *that* thin.

Roos, a former Paralympic wheelchair basketball player, is here to interview him for a Dutch radio programme. Her first question: why has he always been so open about his illness?

"In that way," a deep voice says – Fernando has just changed the female voice on the computer for a male one – "I can show everybody why it is so important to find a medicine."

Fernando is on his proverbial talking chair. He answers every single question. Despite the fact that now he is really looking death in the eye.

"As long as I'm around I keep fighting. But yes, the battle gets more difficult by the day."

"Have you ever had a moment on which you thought: life isn't worth living anymore?" asks Roos.

"Sure. As you can imagine, it's absolutely terrible when you can't do things by yourself anymore. When you can't speak anymore, can't move anymore... When you are forced to eat and drink via a tube... That ain't living anymore. That's trying to survive."

"And what do you do when you've had enough of it all? When you are really depressed?"

"I then close my eyes and listen to music."

"What kind of music?"

"Andrea Bocelli."

"And you enjoy it too?"

"Yes. But I enjoy more things than just music."

"Like what? The current World Cup football tournament for women?"

"Yes. Very much."

"Do you hope that, one day, Isabella will be a very good footballer too?"

"That's my dream. But at the moment she prefers dancing. Do you see what she's wearing?"

"Yes, a tutu."

"I gave it to her yesterday, as a birthday present. And I didn't do that for nothing."

What follows, is one happy smile.

JUNE 22, 2019: **Wig**

As we wait at the reception of the hospice, ready to be picked up, Arthur Numan starts talking about his last visit to Fernando, when he was joined by Lorenzo Amoruso.

"The look in his eyes!" he says.

Turns out that Numan showed up with an enormous wig and funny glasses, as if he was going to a fancy dress party.

"That's the way to deal with Fernando," he adds. "He doesn't like it when you are sad or serious. He wants to be cheered up!"

He shows me a photo. Two photos, actually, the second one

with Fernando sporting the wig.

"Do you see the difference in his eyes? I even told him: 'I don't give a fuck whether you like it or not, 'cos you can't run from me anyway.' That's the kind of humour Fernando likes. And it shows."

Numan knows the hospice by heart. The first time he was here was in 1998, when his Scottish neighbour ended up in one of its beds. Like no other, he knows how important those visits are. That's why he is here to see Fernando for the third time already. And that's why he didn't hesitate when the parents of a young girl with a brain tumor asked him to drop by.

"Seeing me was one of her last wishes. So what do you do when you hear something like that? But it was terrible to see her. A girl like that, barely nineteen, with a head like a balloon... They showed me a photo from a few years earlier, a pic of me and her, taken at the stadium. The difference... Horrible. Five days after my visit she died. It makes you think about the relativity of things. That's why I always encourage people to visit a hospice. After that, you won't go on and on anymore about whether a goal should have been allowed or not."

JUNE 28, 2019: **Step backwards**

They came all the way from Russia, those two diehard fans of The Russian Ultras, Zenit Saint Petersburg's hardcore supporters' group. They wanted to be here at all cost, at the last ever meet & greet with their former hero Fernando Ricksen.

Yes, the last one ever. He's announced it himself, via social media. It's enough, he can't do it anymore. He needs the last little bit of energy for his battle.

Thanks to the Ultras, there have been memorial fireworks near the Zenit stadium already. They also honoured him with an enormous mural. But that wasn't enough. They wanted to be here, in Scotland, to tell him face to face that they will never, ever forget him. Andrey, one of the two: "We are the chosen ones. All the other Ultras paid for our trip."

He tells the story on a small stage, a platform that a bit later will also hold the weight of Nacho Novo and Gordon Smith, Rangers' former Director of Football. There's a crowd of 200.

Front row are Fernando and Veronika. She keeps kissing him. His eyes are glazed. It's obvious: this is the last one.

Fernando then tries to cheer up as Lynsey Glen starts singing *Blue Sea of Ibrox*, but he fails. He can't even push the button of his computer anymore, so a pre-recorded message stays unheard.

And then I see that he can't even cry anymore. So shortly before midnight, he is pushed away and put into the hospice's van, which is waiting outside.

And as he leaves the room, *that* song floats out of the speakers.

"Can you hear the drums, Fernando / I remember long ago another starry night like this / In the firelight Fernando / You were humming to yourself and softly strumming your guitar"

At that point, we all know it's basically over.

JULY 2, 2019: **Exhausted (3)**

"Can't do this any longer."

"What, Fernando?"

"This. Life. Everything."

His messages get shorter and shorter. He hardly replies. He broke contact with his mother, with Victor Morgan and with other close friends. There are constant quarrels with Veronika. He can't pay his bills anymore. The meet & greets are over, so there's nothing to look forward to anymore. His ex Graciela refuses to pay him the enormous amount of money she owes him, despite the fact that a judge ordered her to do so.

There is, in other words, not much left to live for. He is finished. That's probably why he wants to go back to the Netherlands, a country where euthanasia is possible.

I can fully understand it. Every time I visit him, nothing has changed. He is still there, in his bed. On exactly the same spot and in exactly the same position. While, in the meantime, I have been here, there and everywhere. For him, it's the bed – and nothing else. So it's quite understandable that he thinks: let me go to a country where they can terminate this useless life.

JULY 16, 2019: **Cracking jokes**

"A girl realized that she had grown hair between her legs. She got worried and asked her Mom about that hair. Her Mom calmly said: 'That part where the hair has grown is called your monkey. Be proud that your monkey has grown hair.' The girl smiled. At dinner, she told her sister her monkey has grown hair. Her sister smiled and said: 'That's nothing, mine is already eating bananas.'"

I don't believe it. Fernando, who now sports a pretty full beard, is cracking jokes. And he laughs and laughs.

The fighting spirit of this man!!

"Wanna hear another one?"

"Yeah, feel free."

I feel I am relieved. I knew he was sort of crawling up again – hence the porn clips he sent me – but to see him laughing really makes me happy. I heard that some journalists already started writing his obituary. But I think they are too early with that!

I just don't know why he is in this state, at the moment. It's so different from the last time I saw him, at that meet & greet. Is it defeatism? Has he dropped the weapons? Has he stopped trying to become the first person to beat MND?

I don't know. Simply because I don't ask. Can't do that anymore. "Hey Fernando, how are things?" What kind of question is that? What is he supposed to answer, other than his usual 'Top'?

Instead, I point at a postcard on the wall, sent to him by some friends from Fortuna Sittard. Among them his old pal Mark van Bommel. "Keep fighting Fernando!" the card reads. And: "We think of you!"

"One of the best footballers you've ever played with?" I ask him.

"Absolutely."

"Who else? Who is on goal in your All Star Team?"

"Van der Sar."

"Defense?"

"Stam, Skrtel and Numan."

"Midfield, next to Van Bommel?"

"Ferguson, Arteta and Albertz."

"And the attackers?"

"Caniggia, Van Nistelrooij and Arsjavin."

"Quite a team," I app him later, from my hotel room in Glasgow. "But a team needs a good bench too."

Within an hour he answers: "Frank de Boer, Mols, Ronald de Boer, Amoruso, Klos, Van Bronckhorst, Kluivert, Seedorf, Waterreus, Ricksen."

AUGUST 4, 2019: **Tribute**

Five days after his 43rd birthday, which was celebrated with Veronika, Isabella, Ann, Grant, Pauline, Chris and Rachael, the match between his former teams AZ and Fortuna turns into a massive Fernando Ricksen tribute, with chants and banners and applause. I send him a clip of the tv footage.

"Great," he says.

"And did you hear what commentator Frank Snoeks said? 'We all think of you, Fernando!'"

"Yeah, great."

"Of course you are welcome!"

I asked him if I could drop by again. And there I am, once more, at the reception of the St Andrew's hospice in Airdrie. Only this time it doesn't feel good.

The cleaning lady doesn't sing anymore.

The woman behind the desk doesn't ask me about the Netherlands anymore.

The nurse I bump into doesn't greet me, but stares at the floor. And she has something to say to me.

"He is really bad today. You can choose: come back some other time or have a quick look now. One minute, not more."

I decide to do the latter. So I enter his room – and I am shocked. He is totally quiet. The telly is off. There is nothing but silence.

I know I only have sixty seconds, so I ask him what I haven't asked him for months now.

"How are you?"

With one eye closed and one half open, he 'types' a letter.

"T."

He closes both eyes and his head falls forwards.

Ten seconds later he raises his head again, with quite a bit of effort. Once again a letter appears.

"I."

And the same happens again. Eyes, head... And another letter.

"R."

Same routine, in complete silence.

"E."

And a final one, with really a lot of effort.

"D."

And I think: this is the moment. The moment to go. To say goodbye – forever.

I bend over and give him a kiss on the forehead. I then touch his face for the very last time. And I thank him for everything. For all the beautiful moments he has given me – and the world.

SEPTEMBER 7, 2019: **WhatsApp**

WhatsApp from Fernando, via the browser of his computer, to Veronika in Spain.

"See you another time. Bye bye bye."

SEPTEMBER 15, 2019: **Exhausted (4)**

Fernando is asleep.

SEPTEMBER 16, 2019: **Exhausted (5)**

Fernando is asleep.

SEPTEMBER 17, 2019: **Exhausted (6)**

Fernando is asleep.

SEPTEMBER 18, 2019: **The end**

Fernando hasn't woken up since he fell asleep, three days ago. And now, shortly after 10 AM, the last muscles in his body stop working.

He doesn't breathe anymore.

As Veronika calls me with the sad news, I curse and I cry. But at the same time, I am relieved. For him. For her. Because there won't be any suffering anymore.

The fight is over.

Thanks to:

AZ, Bram Bakker, Sepp Blatter, Michiel Blijboom, Gorrit-Jan Blonk, Mark van Bommel, Chantal Borgonovo, Rachael Brown, David Calderwood, Charly Chudik, City Swim Amsterdam, Connal Cochrane, Johan Cruyff Foundation, Beau van Erven Dorens, Gino Facenna, Joy Farquharson, Bernd Fisa, Fortuna Sittard, Rick Geenen, Glasgow Rangers, Lynsey Glen, Pauline Glen, Stan Gordon, Sanne van Haandel, Ann Hamilton, Grant Hamilton, Willem van Hanegem, Klaas Hazenoot, Kevin Hofland, Michiel Holsheimer, Pierre van Hooijdonk, Geert-Jan Jakobs, Stuart James, Mirthe Kleinjans, Roy Knez, KNVB, Hans Koenen, Bert Konterman, Ton Krijnen, Eddy van der Ley, Beverley Lyons, Dieuwertje Mangeng, Robert Marshall, Martin Masset, Chris Mayhead, Jorge Mendes, Rebecca Mennie, Michael Mols, Victor Morgan, Bas van Mulken, Marco Negri, Matthijs van Nieuwkerk, MND Scotland, Nacho Novo, Arthur Numan, One Onlooker, Roos Oosterbaan, Sieb Oostindie, Mari Carmen Oudendijk, Carol Patton, Bobby Petta, Queen Elizabeth University Hospital, Alex Rae, Remco Regterschot, Anneke Ricksen, Isabella Ricksen, Pedro Ricksen, Cristiano Ronaldo, Henk Schiffmacher, Zoë Smith, Esther Startman, St. Andrew's Hospice, Ingrid Stijkel, Kristel Strikkers, Goffe Struiksma, Humberto Tan, Erwin van Tiggelen, Ronald Top, Daniël Valk, Eric Verhoeven, Lauren Verster, Annelot de Vries, Noortje de Vries, John Wallace, Wilma Wallace, Roel Wiche, Wishaw University Hospital, Ineke Zaal, Marcel van der Zee en Zenit Saint Petersburg